D0752845

Frank Sargeant's
Secret Spots

Tampa Bay to
Cedar Key

Florida's Best Saltwater Fishing

by Frank Sargeant

Larsen's Outdoor Publishing

ISBN 0-936513-28-4

Library of Congress 92-74323

Published by:

LARSEN'S OUTDOOR PUBLISHING
2640 Elizabeth Place
Lakeland, FL 33813
(813) 644-3381

PRINTED IN THE UNITED STATES OF AMERICA

9 10

DEDICATION

This book is dedicated to my mom, who sent me off to Lakefork Creek at the age of 10 with a willow pole, a can of worms, and the instructions to bring back supper.

PREFACE

It was a wise angler who pointed out that catching fish is 10 percent knowing HOW to fish, 90 percent knowing WHERE to fish.

This book tackles the second portion of that equation, the 90 percent part. No matter how good your tackle nor how refined your techniques, if you don't know the specific locations where your target species gather, you'll strike out. In some 25 years of chasing Florida's gamefish, I've been blessed with discovering more than my share of good spots-- often as a result of the generosity of good friends and guides, but also because of just plain, dogged persistence.

"If you can't be smart, be stubborn," grandpa Sargeant once told me, and I have.

Are the spots contained in these pages guaranteed to produce, first time, every time?

Naw.

Secret spots are only good sometimes, maybe two hours a day in a particular week in the month of May, on falling tide. If you don't have all that information, your secret spot is not worth the treasure map it's written on. But hit the right place at the right time with the right bait and the right presentation and it's angling heaven. This book gives you as many clues as possible, but you'll have to be smart . . . or stubborn--to put it all together.

A word of caution. Many secret spots remain secret because they're tough to find or tough to get to. This book contains many inshore spots that are risky or downright dangerous to approach if you're not familiar with shallow water operation. Go slowly, go cautiously, and keep your eyes open anytime you   approach an inshore location. Unmarked rocks, bars, pilings and other hazards are part of the flats fishing game, and running at speed in waters you don't know can wipe out your lower unit or even hole your boat in extreme cases. Discretion is definitely the better part of valor in running the inside waters.

Remember, too, that the National Oceanic and Atmospheric Administration Nautical Charts on which the maps are based have in some cases not been updated for 10 years or more. While most areas along the west coast do not see dramatic changes in bottom structure, depths in passes and over bars can alter enough in a matter of days to put you aground. Let your depth finder and your own eyes be the ultimate judge of safe depths, using the charts only as a general guide.

CONTENTS

HOW TO USE THE CHARTS

The charts in this book are based on the offical U.S. government charts produced by the National Ocean Survey. However, because the charts have been sectioned to fit the format of the pages, not all navigation markers and hazards to navigation are shown. And, some charts have been reduced in scale, others expanded, which changes the apparent distances between markers and obstructions. DO NOT DEPEND ON THE CHARTS IN THIS BOOK FOR SAFE NAVIGATION! They are offered only as a guide to good fishing spots.

Key your use of the charts to the seasons. While trout, redfish, snapper and snook are shown well inland in some of the rivers, remember that these locations will produce only in winter, when the fish move inshore to find warmer water. Conversely, species like tarpon and mackerel, shown at the outer edge of the grass flats, will be found there only in temperate weather, spring through fall.

Similarly, areas on the flats showing snook, trout, flounder and reds are likely to produce best on rising or high tides, while swash channels, creek mouths and dredge holes are better bets on low or falling tides.

Adjust your fishing to the seasons, tides and weather conditions, and try a series of the indicated spots until you find action. Remember, no "secret spot" produces every time, but by selecting your spot based on prevailing conditions, you'll frequently find action.

LIST OF CHARTS

(cont'd)

LIST OF CHARTS   (cont'd)

12

ABOUT THE AUTHOR

Frank Sargeant is outdoors editor of the Tampa Tribune and a senior writer for Southern Outdoors, Southern Saltwater and BassMaster magazines. He was formerly an editor for CBS Publications, and a writer for Disney World Publications, as well as southern editor for Outdoor Life. His writing and photos have appeared in a wide variety of other publications, including Field & Stream, Sports Afield, Popular Mechanics, Popular Science and The Reader's Digest. He was a fishing guide before becoming a writer and editor. He holds a masters degree in English and Creative Writing from Ohio University, and has taught writing at the high school and college level. His works have won more than 40 national awards in the past decade. He is also author of the best-selling Inshore Library: THE SNOOK BOOK and THE REDFISH BOOK, THE TARPON BOOK and THE TROUT BOOK. Further information on these books is available in the Resource Directory at the back of the book. Sargeant lives on the Little Manatee River, near Tampa, Florida.

CHAPTER 1

HILLSBOROUGH BAY

The north side of Tampa Bay is actually two sizable bays, separated by Interbay Peninsula. Hillsborough Bay has been heavily impacted by industrial development, and is not a great fishery despite improved water quality--but it has flashes of brilliance and is getting better. Old Tampa Bay, on the other hand, has very good water quality, abundant grass beds, and lots of fish. Let's take a look at Hillsborough Bay first:

THE HILLSBOROUGH RIVER

The Hillsborough River, the bay's main tributary, runs through downtown Tampa. It's an excellent winter snook spot. Fish to 20 pounds hang around many of the bridges and deeper bends and marinas, and are best caught on a slow-trolled live shiner--the same sort of bait used by freshwater bass anglers. They also gang up below the Lowry Park Dam after rainfalls, when strong current occurs there.

Unfortunately, some of the areas where snook are most abundant are also the areas where there are an unusual

Power plants around Tampa Bay put out heated water that attracts trout, snook, reds, snapper, sheepshead and other species from December through March. Jigs or live shrimp fished near bottom produce most of the action.

number of bad guys ashore. It's not advisable to fish from bridges in the Florida Avenue area after dark, and maybe not even in the daytime.

The fishery is probably most intense in winter, but there are some fish in the river year around, particularly around the docks in the lower sections. There's a boat ramp at Tampa City Marina, off Bayshore at the Brorein Bridge.

DOWNTOWN TAMPA

Snook are also fairly abundant in the canals around Davis Islands, where they take a free-lined shrimp or sardine readily. The locals don't welcome visitors in their backyard waterways, but this is public water for boatmen so don't be intimidated.

There are lots of snook in Seddon Channel and the ship basins downtown--pick a morning with lots of wind from the south and fish some of the south-facing seawalls and docks, where bait will be forced up against the cover. A 52-M

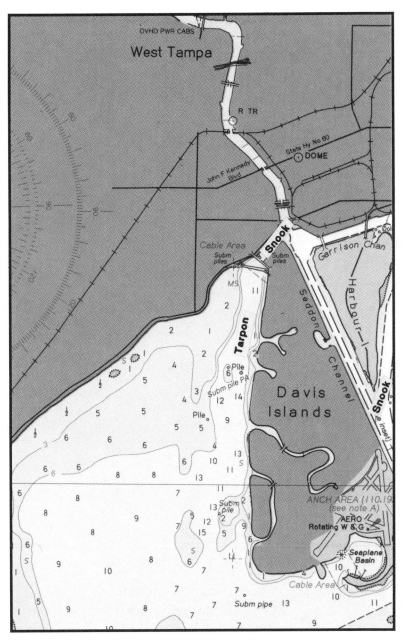

HILLSBOROUGH RIVER AND DAVIS ISLANDS

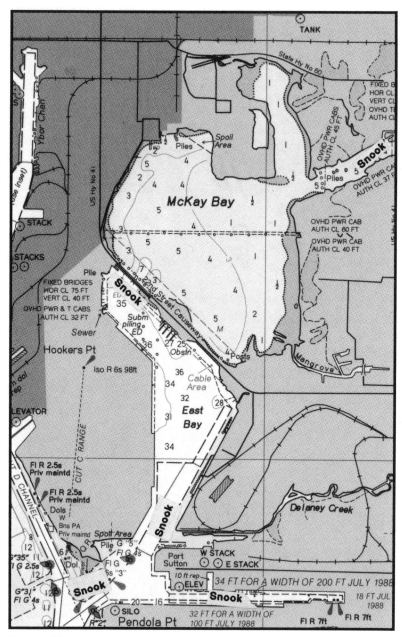

PORT SUTTON AND McKAY BAY

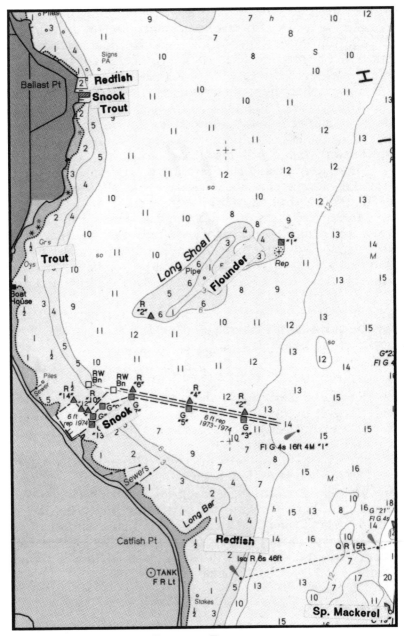

BALLAST POINT TO CATFISH POINT

MirrOlure is a favorite for this action. Trolling live mullet near the seawalls also results in some monster snook. The Port Sutton powerplant outflow is good for snook, jacks, reds and a bit of everything else when it gets cold--and try the rip-rap shoreline to the east for snook early and late.

If you have patience and a compulsion to catch a monster snook in excess of 30 pounds, slow-troll a foot-long ladyfish on 40-pound gear and 7/0 forged hook around the ships in East Bay, the major shipping port, and in Garrison Channel downtown. Summer nights are best for this.

There were once lots of tarpon on the west side of Davis Island in late summer, and a few have been showing up there again in the 8-foot basin in recent years.

McKay Bay turns out reds on occasion--and the nearby Palm River can be very hot for snook when the weather turns cold in late November. Also, the first dam on this river is a good spot to try if a front brings in lots of rain, causing a current flow. Rat-L-Traps, Bangolures and Bomber Long A's are all good.

There are two ramps at the south end of Davis Island, one on the main ship channel, one on the yacht basin, both adjacent the small-plane airport.

BALLAST POINT PIER

For shorebound anglers, this pier is a great facility, thanks in large part to the late Clyde Parrish, who pushed hard to have the extensive artificial reef built there. Today it turns out the same quality snook fishing it did when Clyde walked the boards with his Calcutta pole and 120-pound-test mono.

The reef has attracted sheepshead, reds, snook and trout, and provides good fishing from spring through late fall--and sometimes there are winter runs of trout under the lights. There's a boat ramp and a baitshop/restaurant in the park.

The yacht basin just south of Ballast Point Pier is frequently stacked with small to medium snook--they'll hit live sardines and free-lined shrimp after sundown.

ALAFIA RIVER

The Alafia has gone through tough times, including a massive acid spill in the 1980's that killed most of the fish in

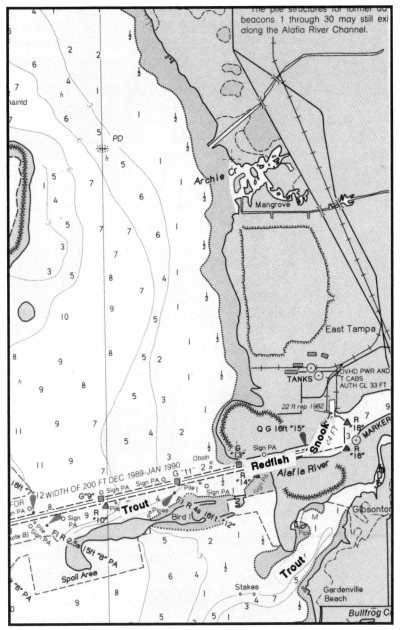

ALAFIA RIVER AND BULLFROG CREEK

21

the lower river. But it has bounced back amazingly well, and these days consistently produces good winter snook fishing from the ship basin near the mouth all the way upstream to the Lithia Springs tributary. Action is particularly good below the rapids near Bell Shoals Road in December, when you can do no wrong with a topwater Rapala or Bangolure.

Try the boatdocks in the lower river from March through early May, and also try the riprap where the deep water from the turning basin turns the corner to shoot out the navigation channel on falling tides.

In spring, there's often a run of trout around the grass on the south side of the river channel, between the channel and the bird islands. Spoons, jigs and live shrimp get them. In winter, fishing live shrimp deep in the ship channel connects with loads of silver trout.

Williams Park, on the north side of the U.S. 41 bridge at Gibsonton, is a good place to launch for fishing up or down river. Bait is available at Giant's Camp, on the south side of the bridge. If you want to fish the upper river for snook, there's a ramp at the Riverview Civic Center, east of U.S. 301 off MacMullen/Booth, another off Vaughn Avenue in Gibsonton.

BULLFROG CREEK

The flats outside Bullfrog Creek have no bullfrogs, but in April and May, these grass patches just south of the Alafia have excellent trout fishing for topwater anglers tossing the Rat-Lure, Bangolure, 7M MirrOlure and similars. Part of the good fishing is in the old channel of the Alafia River, which was cut off by dredging many years gone by. Depths average 3 to 5 feet.

In winter, the Whiskey Stump dredge hole, about a mile south of the mouth of Bullfrog Creek, holds many of those same trout--catch them then on jigs or live shrimp fished deep. The stump hole is not shown on the chart, but it's just north of Whiskey Stump Key, and surrounded by only a foot of water. To get there, you run along the north edge of the Big Bend Power Plant fill, within 20 feet of shore, where there's a dredged channel. The cut exits the main port dredge area just north of Marker 11A.

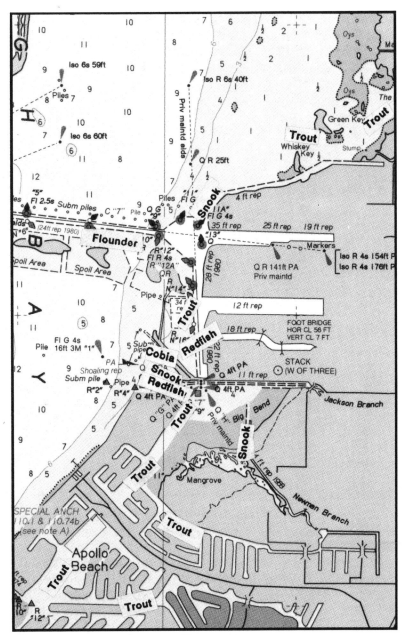

BIG BEND AND APOLLO BEACH

Live sardines, which can be cast-netted on many Tampa Bay grass flats, are a prime bait for snook and most inshore species. The baits are chummed into range with a mix of canned sardines, jack mackerel and whole wheat bread.

BIG BEND

The Big Bend plant itself is always worth a visit in winter. The area has been deeply dredged to accommodate coal barges, thus providing a haven for fish in cold weather. The north basin has water 25 feet deep, the center 12 feet and the south 18 feet, making them all possible refuges for winter spotted trout, silver trout and reds. The deepest part of the port, 34 feet, is just west of Marker 14 in a smaller basin off the main channel. Troll the deep water with jigs by day until you find the fish, or drift along with a weighted shrimp just off bottom. If you don't mind night fishing in cold weather, ease along under the lights after sundown and pitch live shrimp up into the glow. This is a good way to get a wall-hanger trout on occasion.

The entrance channel to the port has rocky bars to the south of it, and the cuts through these bars frequently hold big jacks and sometimes snook. There are always ladyfish and some trout on the flats south of the bars, in about 4 to 7 feet of water. The point of land just south of Marker 12 has numerous rocks and cement slabs, and on high tides there are sometimes big sheepshead and an occasional snook in this area. The water is clear and shallow and the fish are nervous, requiring long casts from a distant boat.

The south side of the powerplant is the outlet side, where water warmed to over 75 degrees comes boiling out into the bay in the millions of gallons daily. Naturally, it creates a fish spa that's usually jammed with snook, baby tarpon, trout, sheepshead, and even cobia from November through February.

The outlet area itself has been closed off to boat traffic because it's a natural draw for manatees, but you can find plenty of fish in the channel outside when it's really frosty.

Also, try the south side of the metal retaining wall, which transmits heat. Often, there are snook huddling right against this wall, as well as small permit which will grab bits of shrimp or crab fished on bottom.

Newman Branch Creek, at the back of the bay where the powerplant is built, sometimes holds snook. The mouth of the creek is a good spot to try on falling water.

Also good are the extensive residential canals of Apollo Beach. Those on the north side of Apollo Beach Boulevard are reached via the entry at the powerplant outflow, while those on the south are accessed via a marked entry channel on the south end of the beach.

Trolling a small jig through the canals is a good way to locate winter trout. You can plug up a snook around the docks here at most anytime of year, but November and early December is the hot time.

The south side has a large boat basin just inside the entry channel, and this area frequently holds seatrout and silvers in winter, along with scads of ladyfish.

There's a public boat ramp on the south side of Apollo Beach Boulevard, which runs west from U.S. 41 at Apollo Beach, and one on the north side, just as the boulevard meets Surfside Drive.

CHAPTER 2

OLD TAMPA BAY

Old Tampa Bay never had the pollution heaped on it that Hillsborough Bay received, and also has had better tidal circulation. As a result, fishing here was never bad, but since the cleanup began in the 1980's, it has become good and sometimes great. Here are some of the productive spots:

INTERBAY PENINSULA

The west side of Interbay Peninsula is making a comeback as water clears and turtle grass grows on what was a denuded sandbar during the years of worst pollution. Coon Hammock Creek and Broad Creek, which run into MacDill Air Base, are excellent spots for winter snook and trout. So is the lower quarter-mile of Picnic Island Creek, just south of Picnic Island Park, though it's so shallow and narrow that you have to be the first boat of the day and have to maintain complete silence to fool the fish.

The flats off Interbay, which were bare sand a few years back, are now growing turtle grass, attracting sizable schools of redfish in fall. Cruise the edge of the bar, looking inland,

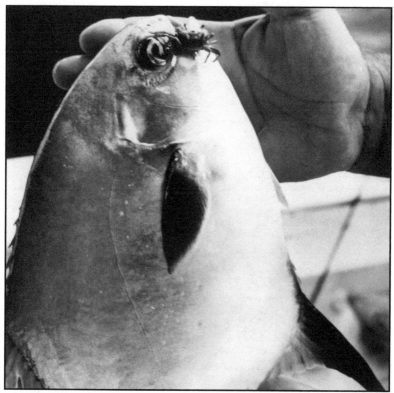

Permit and pompano are common summer catches around the large bridges on Tampa Bay. Most are caught on live fiddler crabs fished close to the pilings.

until you see waking fish, then pole or wade to reach them with gold spoons, topwaters of flyrod streamers.

The south edge of Picnic Island has several holes to about 5 feet that sometimes hold snook in summer. It's strictly live sardine water, and you need a shallow-draft boat to get to them on most tides. Picnic Island Hole, about a half-mile southeast of the point, has depths to 17 feet surrounded by flats only a foot deep. A jig cast into the depths may come up with anything from trout to reds to cobia. There are ramps at Picnic Island Park.

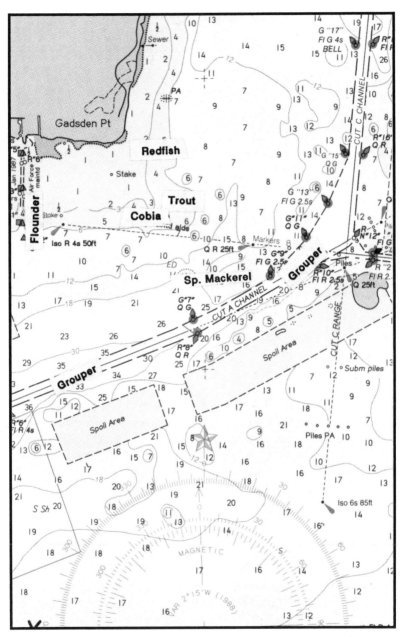

GADSDEN POINT

29

Snook are frequent catches in the passes and sloughs around Weedon Island. Topwaters work early and late, while live sardines are the best bet in brighter hours.

PORT TAMPA

Port Tampa is an ugly, tangled mess of junk metal and rock, but the monster snook love it. Fish to 40 pounds (yep, 40 pounds) are caught here each year by guys with 120-pound test on tuna rods, fishing foot-long ladyfish on forged 7/0 hooks around the trash. Don't bother trying for them with lighter stuff--there's no chance.

There's a rockpile on the flat just north of the port, where you can sneak up and fling a topwater early in the day and usually catch a big trout or maybe a medium-sized snook--or a jack, if nothing else. Locate the pile by the ripple it makes in the current--but watch out that you don't run over it on a higher-than-usual tide. The ramps at the east end of Gandy Bridge are close-by.

THE BIG BRIDGES

Gandy Bridge and nearby Howard Frankland are famous spots for after-dark summer angling for whopper black drum, with fish to 30 pounds taken regularly. Best bet is a medium-sized blue crab fished on bottom on a 5/0 hook and 30-pound or heavier gear. You can also get them on a 1/2 ounce jig with a dark plastic worm tail--crawl it along bottom near the pilings.

Gandy is also a great spot for small permit to about 4 pounds from June through September--live fiddler crabs fished with about 3 to 6 ounces of weight right against the pilings will get them. Chum by scraping off the barnacles from the cement supports. (Gandy Bait and Tackle, on the east end of the Gandy Bridge, often has live crabs and the latest information on what's biting where.)

Both bridges are also good for snook and tarpon after dark, throughout the summer. Shrimp and baitfish gather under the bridge lights en masse, and these attract the gamefish--as well as jillions of ladyfish and catfish.

The deep boat basin and adjoining channel on the southeast end of Gandy is a good winter spot for snook and trout, as well as sheepshead around the rockpiles. It's also good for night snook on topwaters in summer. The Salty Sol Boat Ramp here is one of the best in the Bay area.

The flats on the east side of Old Tampa Bay between Gandy and the Frankland bridge are good trout spots from spring through fall--topwaters, 52-M MirrOlures, and shrimp under a popping cork are all effective. The boat canals cut into Culbreath Isles and other swank developments here are good winter spots for jumbo trout as well as for big snook.

The flats around Courtney Campbell Causeway are frequently good for wading for trout spring through fall, and also hold big reds, particularly in the marshy areas around the east end. The deep bridge span here is a proven spot for big snook after dark.

Some big snook also prowl the boat channel on the north side of the causeway. The docks at the boat ramp have produced some big fish after dark and at dawn in recent years. (This ramp is presently in rough repair--make sure not to drop your trailer wheels over the back edge.)

NORTH OF COURTNEY CAMPBELL

North of the causeway, flats extend out from Double Branch and Rocky Creeks and Cabbage Head Cut, and all of this water can produce trout year around. Fish the flats in

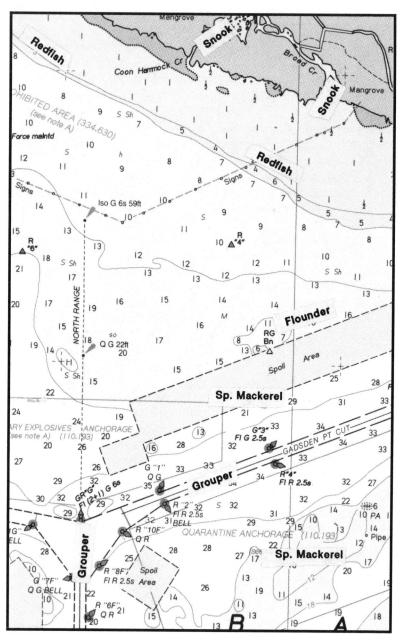

MacDill AFB

32

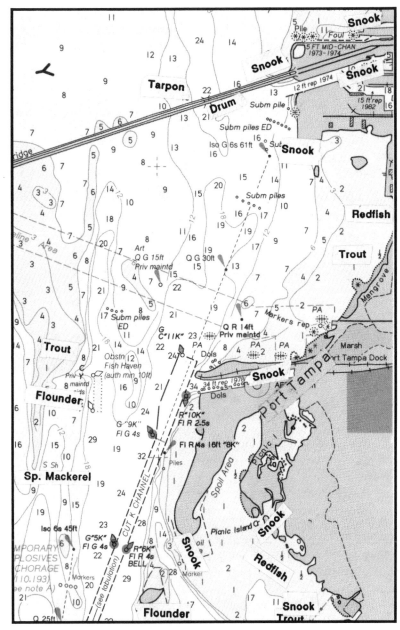

GANDY BRIDGE, PORT TAMPA AND PICNIC ISLAND

temperate weather, the deep creek channels when it gets cold. The approach to Double Branch is extremely shallow, impossible for anything but flats boats or jon boats on low water, but OK in the mid- to high tides; use caution. The slightly deeper sloughs that cut through these shallows, incidentally, are good spots for trout in fall and winter, but you'll probably have to wade to connect because the fish are spooky.

Both creeks are also noted snook producers in winter, and the flats turn out jumbo reds in late summer and fall. You can put in a canoe or jon boat at Upper Tampa Bay Park on Double Branch Creek off Hillsborough Avenue or on Rocky Creek at Rocky Creek Drive and go downstream if you don't want to motor across the open bay from the causeway.

THE WEST SHORE

Snook push into Safety Harbor and hang around the outflow of Lake Tarpon in winter. The deep neck of the harbor, where it meets the main bay, sometimes holds trout on the first winter cold fronts. Phillipe Park, off State Road 590 in Safety Harbor, is the spot to launch.

The dredge holes at the west end of Gandy are good spots for trout and snook in winter--best action is often at dawn on live shrimp. The creeks running into the mangroves north of Gandy turn out snook in March and April.

The deep channel dredged along the south side of the causeway can be a good winter spot for trout, particularly on weekdays when boat traffic is moderate. You can launch a small boat right off the hard sand on the south shore in many places, or if you have a larger boat use the commercial ramps on the west end of the causeway. (Docks in this area, known as Snug Harbor, are worth plugging in summer for linesiders.)

The outflow of the power plant due south of the causeway is an outstanding winter snook spot, but you have to be the first boat there in the morning and make a quiet approach. The water is very shallow on the flats surrounding the channel, and only about 4 feet deep in the channel, so it takes caution to avoid spooking the fish. Slip in on the push pole, anchor, and work over the flow and the first 200 yards of the run with a Bangolure or 5M MirrOlure, or a live shrimp or pinfish.

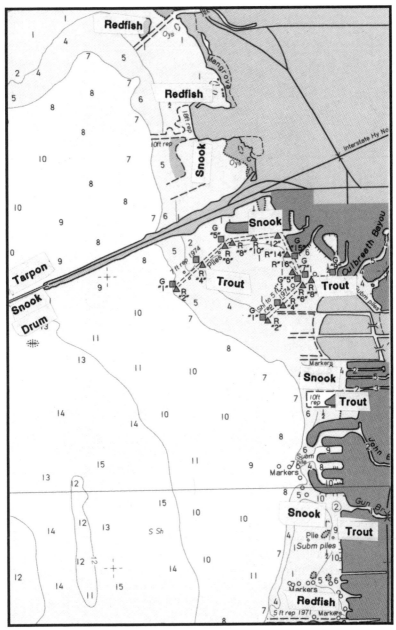

CULBREATH ISLES AND HOWARD FRANKLAND BRIDGE

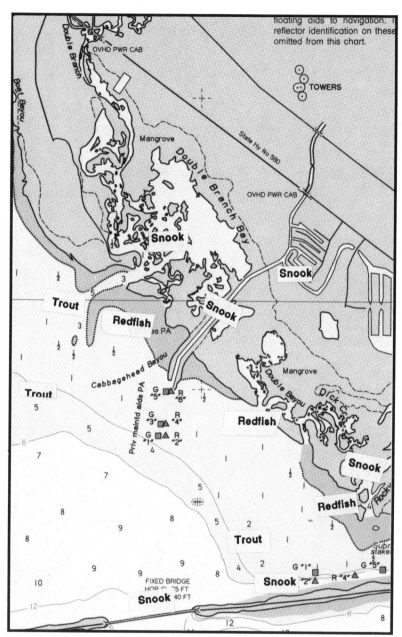

ROCKY CREEK TO DOUBLE BRANCH

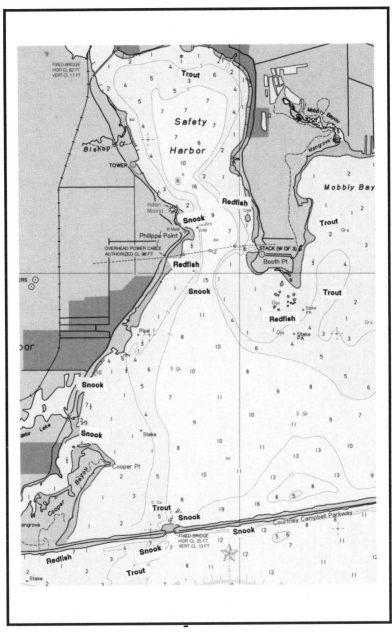

SAFETY HARBOR TO COURTNEY CAMPBELL CAUSEWAY

The shoreline running east from the powerplant often holds snook in spring and fall--spooky fish that see lots of lures, but skilled anglers like Captain Russ Sirmons fool them with live sardines.

Go around the corner to the entry basin of the power plant, where you'll find water deep enough to float the fuel barges, and good winter trout, snook and sheepshead action. There are some jumbo snook in this area, and they're susceptible to a 10-inch mullet drifted deep around the seawalls. (Leave your 4-pound test at home.)

WEEDON ISLAND

The grass flats running south along the shore of Weedon Island are a reserve where outboard motors are not allowed near shore, and fish have taken advantage of this protection. Pole, drift or wade the area from spring through fall and you'll find plenty of jumbo redfish and snook. The reds like to settle into the deeper sloughs between islands, about 100 yards offshore. Snook like the yellow holes closer in, plus deeper cuts between the islands.

Christmas Pass, the deepest of these cuts, is outstanding on falling water on weekdays. There's a little slough inside, to the south, where snook sometimes gather on lows--wade to it. Work south on the outside around Papy's Point and you'll often see snook in the holes. Again, they're nervous.

Bayou Grande and Riviera Bay are both very good snook spots, though it generally takes live sardines to fool the hard-pressed fish--concentrate on points and bars on the rise, canal mouths on the fall. Boat docks are good after dark pretty much year around here. The public park, accessed off the west side of the Gandy causeway, provides shore access, and some nice fish are caught by waders on weekdays--too busy on weekends most of the time. The park intersects the point where the two bays meet, and there's a strong tide flow which snook enjoy.

The shoreline channel between Venetian Isles and Smacks Bayou always holds some snook. The mouth of Smacks Bayou is a good place to drift a live shrimp or sardine on falling tide, and the 18-foot deep hole at the mouth sometimes holds

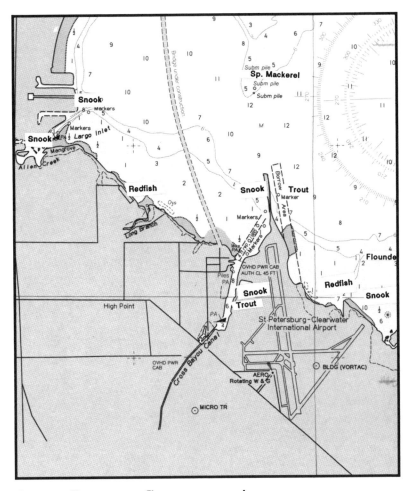

ALLEN CREEK TO CLEARWATER AIRPORT

winter trout, as does the 10-foot water just to the south in Snell Isle Harbor.

Coffepot Bayou averages 6 feet deep, with holes to 11 feet, and holds snook year around. There are ramps at Coffeepot Park, off 4th Street, and at Crisp Park, off 35th Avenue Northeast.

The Pier in downtown St. Petersburg can be a good spot for Spanish mackerel in spring and fall, at least whenever

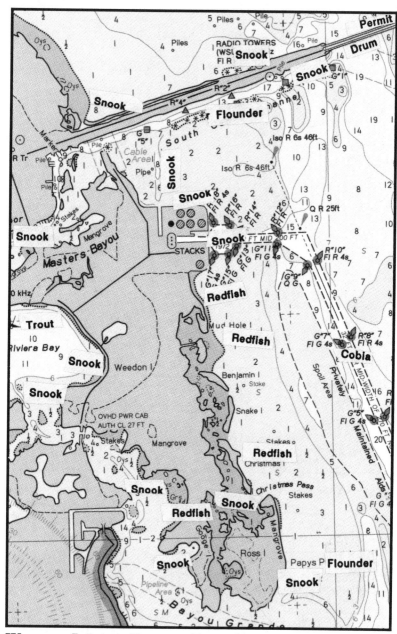

WEEDON ISLAND, RIVIERA BAY AND BAYOU GRANDE

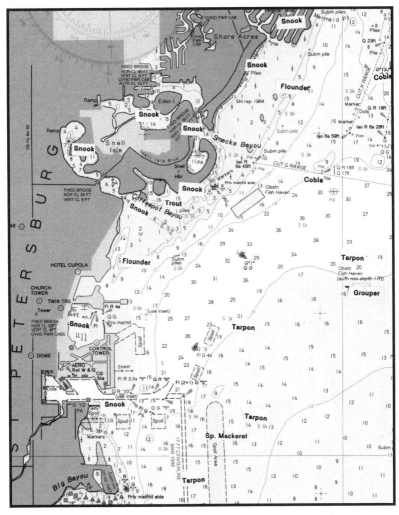

VENETIAN ISLES TO ST. PETERSBURG

baitfish schools come within casting range. There are usually sheepshead around the pilings, and they'll take fiddler crabs fished very close to the cement.

In late summer, the 20-foot-waters about a half-mile off the pier and around the sweep of Pinellas Point are a noted area for big tarpon. They're caught by chumming with cut

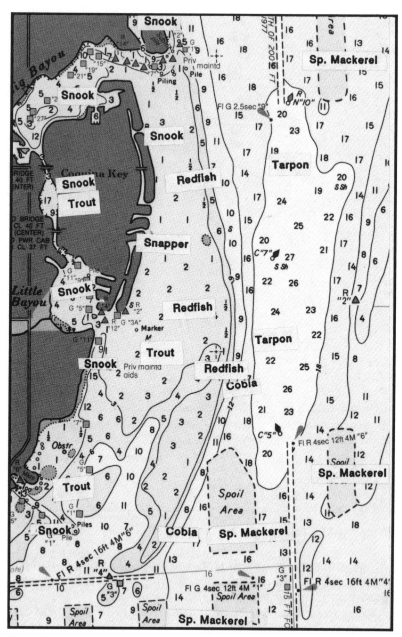

BIG BAYOU, LITTLE BAYOU AND PINELLAS POINT

menhaden, and fishing a whole menhaden on bottom on heavy gear. Motor around the area until you see rolling fish, then anchor and put out your chum, along with a spread of baits on 40-pound-gear. Take along your catfish repellent.

DOWNTOWN ST. PETERSBURG

The entrance to the North Yacht Basin is worth a few tosses on falling water for snook spring through fall. Noisy topwaters at dawn and dusk work well when the fish are there.

The Municipal Pier has sheepshead around the pilings most of the year, and an occasional run of Spanish mackerel comes within range when the bait approaches.

The dredge holes around Whitted Airport, south of the Pier, offer depths to 25 feet where you can connect with spotted trout in winter, as well as silvers, sheepshead and drum. The entrance to Bayboro Harbor has 20-foot depths, and is worth trolling with a jig or diving plug to locate schools of winter fish. Nearest ramp is at Grandview Park, at 6th Street and 39th Avenue South.

PINELLAS POINT

The bar running from Big Bayou to Point Pinellas brings 10 feet of water right up against foot-deep flats, backed with plenty of turtle grass. It's a natural area for trout and reds, and the water is usually clear enough to make artificials productive. Keep an eye to the east as you drift these flats, because you may see big tarpon rolling in the deep water just off the bar.

The shoreline just south of the mouth of Little Bayou has 10 feet of water and more, and often holds sizable snook, particularly when most of the water has fallen off the surrounding flats.

The flats due south of Pinellas Point have lots of grass, intersected by unpredictable deepwater cuts. It's a very fishy area, more than a mile wide and flushed regularly with lots of clear Gulf water and live bait. Drift the 4- to 6-foot depths where the grass is most plush, tossing topwaters or slow-sinkers. For shorebound anglers, the mile-long sweep of the Clam Bar invites wading out to where the trout action is best.

The channel markers about two miles southeast of Point Pinellas often hold cobia in spring. The spoil bars south of the main ship channel are excellent places to anchor and chum for big mackerel, while the dredged cut itself turns out nice grouper for those trolling big diving plugs on downriggers. The channel averages 35 feet deep, giving about a 7- to 10-foot relief from the surrounding bottom. This rocky edge holds not only gag grouper but occasional schools of jumbo mangrove snapper, these best caught on live sardines fished on heavy leads.

Also of interest adjacent the main ship channel are the spoil areas just inside the Skyway, where schools of whopper sheepshead gather in March to spawn. Fish bottom with live fiddlers, shrimp or tubeworms to get them.

There's a boat ramp near all of the above at Bay Vista Park, off Pinellas Point Drive.

CHAPTER 3

LOWER TAMPA BAY

The southeast shore of Tampa Bay offers fine fishing despite the heavy development on the north and west shores of this vast estuary, Florida's largest bay and busiest shipping port.

The south shore has a shoal along its entire length, extending up to a half-mile from the mangrove shoreline, and on this shoal there are frequent grass beds, with more growing all the time thanks to recent quality improvements in the water coming from the upper bay. The habitat creates good fishing for snook and reds, sometimes for trout, and seasonally for cobia.

LITTLE MANATEE RIVER

The Little Manatee River is one of Florida's cleanest and best, and has good fishing throughout its length from November through early March for snook, reds and trout. The fish gather in deep bends and holes, and around creek mouths on falling water. There's a heavy November bite on glass minnows as far up as the railroad trestle (a good night snook spot), and you can connect during this feed with very small silver-tailed jigs or small mackerel flies. Fish the creek mouths with noisy topwaters for snook, or troll deep divers in the bends--the "Cemetery Hole" is one of the deepest areas, and a good spot for a lunker.

The river splits into three channels in its final mile or so. The north channel is the main navigation route, usually too busy to hold a lot of fish. The center channel has a fairly deep pool down its middle, and this is a good area to drift for trout in winter. Trout and snook also come up the south channel in winter, providing good fishing at the old bridge to Goat Island among other spots.

In summer, many of the deep holes in the river hold small tarpon, anywhere from a foot long up to about 30 pounds. They're not easy to catch on artificials, but will often take a free-lined sardine or shrimp. Fish them where you see them rolling.

At the mouth of the river, the bay on the east shore of Sand Key is a good spot to drift for trout much of the year-- depths average 4 to 6 feet. The east shoreline of this key is deep and a likely snook spot on falling water. This deep water forms a Y just north of the island, creating two channels through flats only a foot deep--a good place to visit on spring lows. The ramp at Shell Point Fish Camp, off Shell Point Road in Ruskin, is nearest this area.

BAHIA BEACH

The south basin at Bahia Beach holds winter trout, sheepshead and drum. Live shrimp on bottom gets them. The main entry channel, on the north side of the condos, leads into a large sailboat harbor at Bahia Beach Resort. There's a ramp on the harbor.

Just before the channel opens to the harbor, there's a narrow cut making off to the east, and if you follow this cut it leads to a deep basin where snook sometimes gather in cold weather.

The cuts in E.G. Simmons Park, just north of Ruskin, are good spots for winter trout and reds, and you can often catch them from shore on shrimp or jigs. There's a good ramp here, but the access to the open bay is shallow.

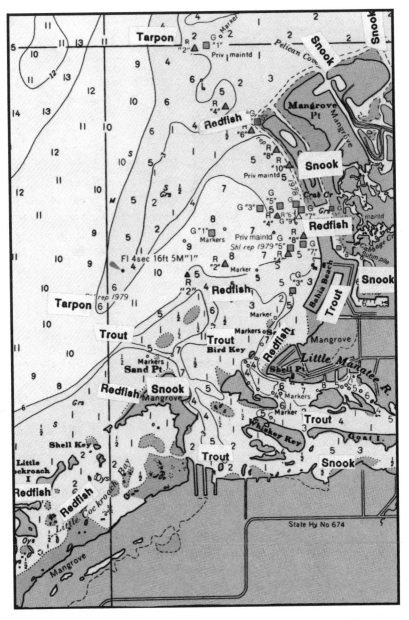

BAHIA BEACH, LITTLE MANATEE RIVER AND LITTLE COCKROACH BAY

The shallows from Piney Point southward offer abundant creek mouths where action on snook and reds can be good on falling water. On the rise, fish the deeper mangrove edges and inside the creeks.

LITTLE COCKROACH BAY

Little Cockroach Bay, just south of the mouth of the Little Manatee, is extremely shallow and littered with oyster bars. It's mostly limited to john boat traffic or wading anglers because of the shallows, but it holds fair numbers of reds and snook throughout the warmer months.

There are deep exit passes between most of the larger islands, and each of these is a likely location on falling water. Big Pass, just north of the Cockroach Bay entry, is the best known of these little cuts, and the easiest to reach. The fish get lots of pressure, though--live sardines fished on weekdays by waders do best. Fish the outside of the islands on rising water for redfish.

There's a grassy slough just inside the very shallow and frequently barren bar at the outer edge of the flat running from the Little Manatee to Port Manatee, and this whole area frequently holds nice reds and some keeper snook. They hit best if you get out and wade on low tide, casting to the deeper holes.

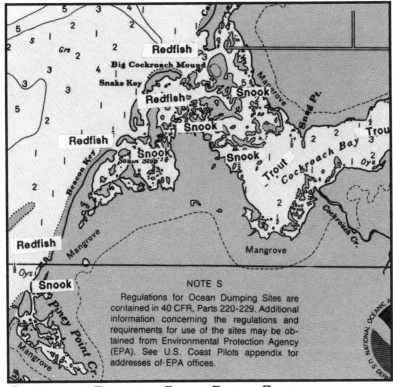

COCKROACH BAY AND PINEY POINT CREEK

COCKROACH BAY

Cockroach Bay is a wonderful fishery from spring through late fall. There are dozens of little mangrove islands cut by clear flats and occasional potholes, and the entire area is worth fishing by wading or poling a shallow draft boat. The islands south of the marked entry channel hold lots of fish and don't get much pressure.

The entry channel itself frequently produces, especially on the fall, when live sardines will catch snook, reds and big trout, particularly after dark. (This dark green channel winds past the Cockroach Bay ramp, a good, paved ramp with quick access from U.S. 41--but vandalism of your vehicle is a possibility here after dark.)

There are deep exit passes between most of the larger islands, and each of these is a likely location on falling water. Fish the outside of the islands on rising water for redfish.

The oyster bars at "Hole in the Wall", the entry to Cockroach Bay proper, are a good spot to cast topwaters or slow-sinkers for snook after dark on rising water. There are also potholes near the north side of the island in the bay where snook sometimes gather on low water. You'll have to wade to fool them, except after dark. Drift and cast the open bay for trout in the fall and spring on high water.

On the outside, there's a spring run of big silver trout into the hole just north of the mile-long sandbar that juts out from the Cockroach entry channel. Fish bottom with live shrimp or small jigs to get them.

PINEY POINT AND PORT MANATEE

From Piney Point northward (there's a dirt ramp at the point where you can launch a small boat) there are numerous grass beds, always good for several trout on topwaters or live sardines as the tide rises. Moody Point Creek, marked by a white sandbar at it's mouth, is a good spot to try on a falling tide--run in to the south, beach your boat and walk silently along the beach to fish this narrow spot. You can also catch

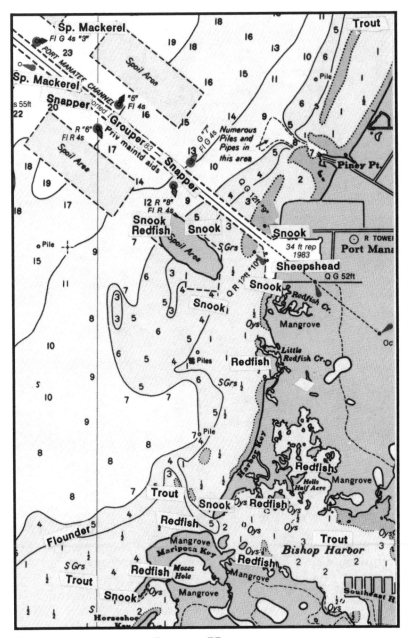

PORT MANATEE TO BISHOP HARBOR

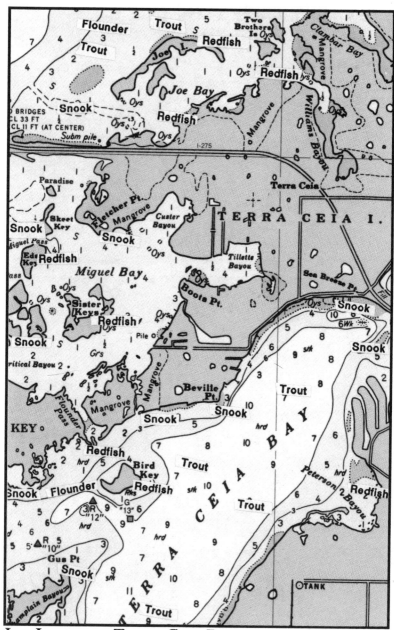

JOE ISLAND TO TERRA CEIA BAY

52

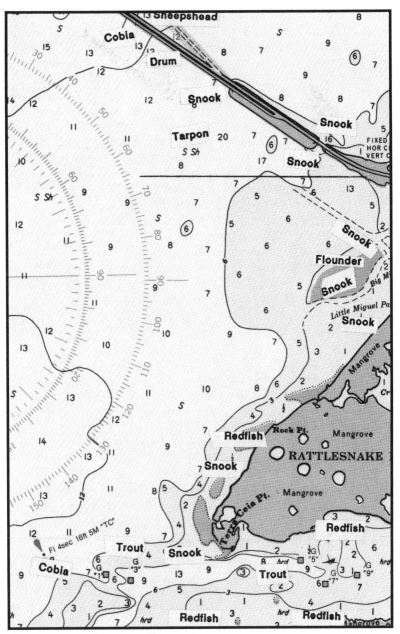

SKYWAY TO TERRA CEIA POINT

53

some snook and reds by working inside the creek itself on high water, but they're spooky in there.

There are usually snook and reds in the 4-foot deep pockets south of the Port Manatee spoil island, as well.

The entire north shore of the spoil island is a noted snook spot from May through September, and a great area for bull reds August through October. The western tip of the island is an incredible snook hole on falling water--anchor there, or get out and wade along the shoreline, tossing live sardines, pinfish, finger mullet or Baitrunner mullet imitations. Hundreds of big linesiders are caught here each summer.

Also in summer, the port itself holds a train-load of monster linesiders and big redfish. They usually gather in the areas where the dredged holes run into the flats, creating shallows where they can trap bait. The Zara Spook is a deadly lure for these fish, as is the Rat-Lure.

There are spoil bars on both sides of the channel near the range marker west of the island, and these are excellent areas to anchor and chum for big Spanish mackerel in spring and fall. Live sardines do the job, but so do fast-moving spoons and chrome Rattletraps. Check the range markers for cobia in spring.

Rocky areas of the channel are also very good for mangrove snapper, seabass and an occasional nice grouper. Work right down the edge of the channel via depthfinder, dropping live sardines to the ledges. Jigs also work, but not so well as the sardines for big snapper.

On falling water, the culvert on the south edge of the port facility is worth a few casts.

Redfish Creek, just south of the spoil island at Port Manatee, requires high water to get into, but it's deep once you're inside. It's a good snook spot, but you have to be the first boat there and you have to be absolutely silent to connect. Fish the deep hole at the mouth on the fall.

BISHOP'S HARBOR AREA

Just north of Bishop's Harbor is Little Redfish Creek, which has a deep hole at it's mouth where snook gather on outgoing tide. The creek branches just inside the first island, with one branch going back out to the bay--sometimes good for medium snook--the other winding through the mangroves off to the south. It looks fishy, but I've never caught anything on the south branch.

Bishop's Harbor is a fishery in its own right, and is worth a full day of quiet poling. There are numerous oyster bars, deep mangrove shorelines and creeks, and you're likely to encounter reds and snook in any of these locations.

On falling water, the main outlet channel is the place to be. Anchor or get out and wade along the sand bank and cast to the channel, which is as much as 5 feet deep--good spot to drift an unweighted shrimp or sardine. It often holds nice flounder in addition to snook, reds and trout. The water is clear--don't crowd the fish or you'll strike out. Bishops Harbor ramp, at the end of Bishops Harbor Road east from U.S. 41, provides access.

NEAR THE SKYWAY

Mariposa Key, south of the entry to Bishop's, has a deep shoreline, and frequently attracts schools of reds spring through fall--the area is a favorite of Captain James Wood. The outflow from Clambar Bay, adjacent, is a good spot to anchor on a falling tide and fish for passing snook and reds. Sand bottoms here often turn out flounder.

There's a series of holes reaching southwest all the way to Joe Island, with water as deep as 5 feet on low tide, where you're likely to catch trout in the middle, reds and snook along the edges.

There's a narrow cut between the Skyway causeway and the island, and this can be a good spot on a falling tide for snook, reds and flounder. Potholes behind the island in the area of Joe Bay also hold snook and reds.

The outside edge of the bar from the Skyway to Port Manatee can be a spot for schools of jumbo reds to cruise August through October, and you may see cobia along this bar anytime from April to October. Troll a small gold spoon where the bar falls off to about 4 feet and you'll catch some lunker flounder, as well.

CHAPTER 4

FISHING THE SUNSHINE SKYWAY

The world's longest fishing pier is no place for those who don't wear hiking shoes. With the new South Pier now in operation at the Sunshine Skyway, there's more than two miles of bridge available, including the 8,400-foot south side and 3,360 feet on the north. The piers are so long that you can literally walk to offshore fishing for such deepwater species as grouper and king mackerel.

In fact, this pier is so long that some anglers take their tents and stay overnight, figuring it's just too darned far to walk for one day of fishing.

The bridge has unique advantages over beach piers, because it spans the main entrance to Tampa Bay. Enormous amounts of water pour through the span with each tide change, and with it comes tons of baitfish, and all the species that eat them.

Depending on the season, the bridge is likely to produce anything from 150-pound tarpon to 30-pound king mackerel and 60-pound cobia. It's famed as a spot for heavyweight snook, and also turns out reds to 30 pounds and more in fall. And for light tackle anglers, there's no better spot to tangle with Spanish mackerel. Meat fishermen find plenty of sheepshead from fall through spring, and the addition of the new reefs, now being built from bridge rubble, should make the area a hotspot for gag grouper, mangrove snapper and sea bass, among other bottom feeders.

The Florida Department of Transportation has been working on converting the lower portions of the bridge to a fishing pier since 1983. The job is now completed, and both sides now provide lots of good parking, safe entry and exit to the four-lane, and the much-appreciated public toilets. There are even vending machines.

And things will get even better in the near future. The north-south lanes on each side will be connected via a U at their ends, making it possible for anglers to drive to their favorite fishing spots, turn around at the end and return to shore without the long walk now needed to reach the more distant spots. Anglers can park right on the bridge and fish out the windows of their cars when the job is completed.

FISHING THE SEASONS

What you catch on the Skyway depends on the season, as well as what part of the span you chose to probe. In summer, it's prime time for tarpon to 150 pounds. At times, hundreds of the big silver kings can be seen rolling around the baitfish schools.

There's also good action on jumbo snook to 30 pounds through the summer, mostly after dark, and in early fall schools of giant reds pass through. There's plenty of bait around the bridge throughout the summer, and plenty of Spanish mackerel under them.

THE NORTH PIER

The North Pier is generally more productive of snook because water 9 to 12 feet deep sweeps by the point where the causeway meets the bridge span there, creating a strong current with lots of eddies that always hold baitfish.

58

The Sunshine Skyway Fishing Pier is the world's longest, and provides a shot at everything from king mackerel and tarpon to sheepshead and snook.

The drop to the 20- to 24-foot depths of the open bay is also nearer the causeway on the north end, and the abrupt topography lends itself to an assortment of mangrove snapper, sea bass and gag grouper, particularly on the very rapid drop from 15 to 20 feet. The bridge spoil reefs in the 20-foot zone are also excellent for grouper, and the upwellings they create are prime spots for kings, Spanish and tarpon.

Also on the north side is the Bunces Pass Bridge, a midget compared to the Skyway proper, but a very productive spot for night snook in summer. Live sardines or pinfish anchored to bottom are the classic technique.

The shoal on the southwest side of the Bunces Pass Bridge is wadable on most tides, and will put you in reach of snook, reds and sometimes trout prowling the north-south dredged boat channel.

THE SOUTH PIER

The South Pier is longer than the north, but travels over flatter terrain. It's about 7 feet deep where the span leaves the causeway, and stays that depth for over 3/4 mile before dropping into an area where depth varies rapidly from 13 up to 10 and back down to 14 feet before falling into the 20-foot depths of the main bay. This area, which begins within about a half-mile of the point where the bridge curves north from its initial northwest course, is good for mackerel, kings and a bit of everything else.

While the main piers provide all the fishing anybody could want, smart snook anglers don't ignore the smaller spans on both the north and south ends. On the north side, the lighted bridge over Bunces Pass has close to 15 feet of water below it, and is an excellent spot to connect with big snook after dark. The smaller bridge just south of the toll booth passes over shallower water, but also holds snook and lots of sheepshead in winter.

On the south end, there's only one added bridge available to anglers and it's a small one, but depth is 16 feet down the chute, and on a falling tide snook stack up there to feed, along with ladyfish, jacks, redfish and a bit of everything else at times. The trick is to stand on the downtide wing, throw uptide under the span with a big wobbling plug like a Bomber Long A, Magnum Rapala or a Cisco Kid and bring it back just slightly faster than the current. Work it so that it swings past you, increasing in speed at the end of the drift as it comes across the current. Use heavy gear and hang on--the fish tend to be as long as your leg, and they know where the pilings are. (If they won't hit plugs, toss them a jumbo live shrimp.)

SKYWAY TACKLE

To connect with the pier heavyweights, the big-shouldered tarpon and smoker kings, it's essential to use very heavy gear. Bridge regulars use 80-pound gear and fighting belts, and even at that they often lose fish, either to runs that last longer than their line capacity or to a hitch around one of the pilings.

Spanish mackerel are a common Skyway catch from spring through fall. Small spoons, jigs and live sardines are all effective. Fish near the baitfish schools that usually hang close to the span.

Most bridge regulars use live threadfins from spring through fall. Castnets make it easy, but the baitfish can be jigged up right in the fishing area by lowering down a chain of number 12 gold hooks and twitching them slightly. (Owner has a "Bait Maker" chain with six hooks already made up for this purpose.) You can keep the baits alive in a battery-aerated bucket on the bridge, or lower them down in a vented baitbucket on a cord.

They're fished on 39-pound-test copper wire and 2/0 hooks with a trailer for the kings, or on a single forged 5/0 at the end of a length of 100-pound-test mono for the tarpon. Most experts like to add a bit of chum to bring fish to their baits, either by lowering a chum block in a mesh bag or by snipping up threadfins. With the tarpon, it's always wise to keep an eye out for rolling fish and get your bait into their area promptly, since the schools move around often.

Sometimes the fish bite best on baits trailed at the surface, other times it takes several ounces of lead to drop it down into the strike zone--vary the weight if you're not getting bit.

Big Spanish and blues also hit the threadfins, but the fun way to catch them is to stand on the uptide side of the bridge and make long casts with 8-pound-test gear and a 1/8 to 1/4 ounce jig or silver spoon. Bring the lure back in long, rapid whips of the rod, and the fish will let you know if they're around. (The baitfish usually gather on the uptide side of the bridge as well, and you'll do best if you center your fishing close to these schools, revealed by the "showers" they create on the surface.)

Here, as anywhere else, you have to match your tackle to the water, present the bait naturally and in the proper stratum of the water column, and keep moving until you find where the fish are.

This is to say, if you're after tarpon, walk until you see them rolling before you make a cast. If you want Spanish, find the baitfish and toss fast lures or live baits. For sheepshead, you need to get your bait slap up against the pilings--and you'll do a whole lot better with fiddlers or tubeworms than with shrimp. And so on. Move, look, think--and be ready to change your angling style quickly if a target of opportunity-- such as a cobia with pinfish on its mind--cruises by.

If you're fishing for meat as well as sport, you need to make a bridge net or a bridge gaff part of your gear. If you hook up with a fish a mile out on the span, it's unlikely you'll be able to successfully walk him all the way back to the causeway where you can beach him, so the landing gear on a dropcord is essential.

O'Neill's Bait House, on the north side at the last exit before the toll booth, is a handy place to get bait, ice and tackle, and it has a free ramp that's open 24 hours. Maximo Park, just north of O'Neills, also has a good ramp, but is open only during daylight hours. Skyway Jack's, also at the north exit, makes some of the best breakfasts in the Bay area. A ramp is also in the works for the south end of the Skyway, at the South Pier exit.

CHAPTER 5

MORE BRIDGE ACTION IN TAMPA BAY

From June through August each year, thousands of young permit, 2 to 4 pounds, pour into Tampa Bay. They travel in large, rambunctious schools, and feed anywhere they can find crabs, barnacles and other crunchies.

Among their favorite feeding stations, first discovered by Tampa angler extraordinaire James Wisner several decades ago, are the big bridges that span the western arm of the bay, between St. Petersburg and Tampa.

Here, three major bridges--the Gandy, the Howard Frankland and the Courtney Campbell Causeway--connect the two major metro areas with spans ranging up to five miles long.

They're also found around the Sunshine Skyway Bridge, which stands at the mouth of the bay. The Skyway offers some nine miles of pilings, plus the world's longest fishing piers, the remnants of the old bridge.

The permit begin to show around the pilings when the water temperature reaches 82 to 84 degrees, usually in mid-June. The action remains good throughout the summer, though the fish often migrate from bridge to bridge and make it appear as though they've left to the casual angler.

You can occasionally catch permit on shrimp and jigs, but if you're serious about catching them, the only bait worth bothering about is the fiddler crab.

CRAB ROUNDUPS

Most locals catch their own. They have "fiddler round-ups" which employ several anglers. Working the shores of tidal creeks or shallow bayside beaches, they readily find colonies of hundreds of the arm-waving fiddlers. The trick to catching them is to herd them into a funneled-down area created by holding several sheets of plywood or cardboard against the sand, and then scooping them up with a net or bucket, or with gloved hands. (Fiddlers can't bite very hard with their single large pincher, but it's enough to hurt at times.)

The baits are stored in a bucket with a half-inch of water in the bottom, and with a bit of net or screening added for them to climb out on. Putting too much water in the bucket will cause them to drown quickly as they use up the available oxygen, but if they can get above the water and are kept out of the sun, they'll live for days.

The crabs are small, about thumbnail-sized on the average. It's a good idea to remove the pincher as they're baited, not because of the danger but because a fish often grabs the waving arm and pulls the bait off the hook.

Size 1 or 2 light wire hooks are used, necessary both because of the delicate baits and the small mouth of the fish. The hook is slipped into the back corner of the shell and out the side.

BOAT POSITIONING

A major part of successfully fishing the bridges is boat positioning. Fishing 20 feet of water, it's necessary to drop anchor at least 100 feet uptide from the pilings to get reason-

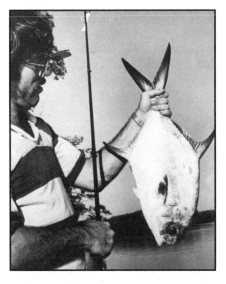

Permit, usually thought of as a flats species found only in the tropics, are frequent visitors to Tampa Bay in mid-summer when water temperatures exceed 85 degrees. Anglers chum by scraping barnacles from bridge pilings, and catch the tasty scrappers with thumbnail-sized fiddler crabs.

able holding power. The idea is to back down until the boat hangs right beside the pilings.

A line is then passed around the upright; bumpers put in place prevent the boat from rubbing against the structure.

Obviously, this is not something that can be done in rough water. Forget it if there's wind greater than 10 knots, less than that in some exposed locations, or when wind and tide oppose each other. If there's more than a light chop, the boat will knock itself to splinters against the bridge.

Fishing is best when the tide flow is strong, either incoming or outgoing. Any piling is likely to hold fish, but the few guides who fish the bridges say they often set up on the last piling on the downtide side of the bridge, so that hooked fish will be fought in the open water behind them rather than right up against the pilings.

GET CHUMMY

Most bay bridges are in pairs, one for each direction of traffic, and the most productive spots are on the lower side of the up-current span. The reason is that chum is a major part of the game plan, and the chum needs to go through nearby pilings to be most effective.

The chum is not portable. It's found right on the pilings, in the form of barnacles, crabs and other miniature edibles clustered there. Just like sheepshead fishermen, permit anglers chip off this accumulated growth into the moving tide, creating a mix of meat and shell that stretches for several hundred feet to draw in the fish.

RIGGING RIGHT

Most of the permit seem to hold within a few inches of the bottom, so that's where the bait has to be presented. Getting it down there in a 4-knot current takes lots of weight. Egg sinkers up to 3 ounces are used to do the job. Twenty-pound gear is about right. The heavy line also prevents the edges of the big sinker from cutting through the mono. The weight is kept away from the hook by a barrel swivel, below which 18 inches of 30-pound-test leader runs to the eye.

The crab is hooked up and lowered straight down, the reel in free-spool so the bait hits bottom quickly. Lowering it slowly tends to make it "balloon" outward in the current, and the fish seem to hit best close to the pilings.

Even with a 3-ounce weight, the bait does not stay on bottom more than a few seconds as the current puts a belly in the line and eventually kites it up into the water column.

The trick to getting bit is to lightly tap the sinker against bottom, raising it only a couple of inches and then dropping it quickly. The bite--often only a light tap--usually comes as the bait is being raised.

If nothing takes and the sinker loses contact, the angler free-spools a bit more line to sink it back to bottom, where he can get in a few more bounces. But even then, it's usually necessary to reel in and make another drop at least once a minute--this is not casual fishing.

It's also necessary to keep a sharp eye out for weeds or moss gathering on the line. Whatever hits the line, even at the surface, quickly shoots down the length of it to drape sinker and bait in vegetation. Even a small bit will keep the permit from taking.

It takes a sharp hookset to drive the hook home despite the large weight and the strong tides, but if you succeed, you're immediately rewarded with a line-zipping run that will convince you you've tied into something much bigger than the fish usually turns out to be. The fish know how to take advantage of the strong tide to fight to the last. On the typical permit gear used on the flats--light spinning gear and 8-pound-test--it's doubtful if a single fish could be landed around the bridges. The heavier tackle takes its toll, though--most give up in a few arm-wrenching minutes.

Small permit are absolutely delicious on the table, and because of the nature of the fishery here, it does no harm to take a couple home. There's no bag limit on fish smaller than 20 inches because of the difficulty of distinguishing them from the very similar and closely related pompano--and no gourmet can tell the difference on the platter, either, except that maybe the permit might be just a bit firmer and tastier.

There's no directed permit fishery inshore in the Bay area for mature fish, except for a rare arrival of stray schools around Passage Key bar, at the mouth of the bay during spring and early summer. Thus, it does no harm to keep a few for the table.

CHAPTER 6

BEYOND THE SKYWAY

The waters outside the Sunshine Skyway offer tremendous angling opportunities for just about everything that swims in the Gulf. There's an abundance of both inshore and deep-water species, lots of clear water, lots of bait, and always a lee shore where you can fish if the wind kicks up-- though, to be sure, those lees are a lot more abundant for easterly winds than for westerlies.

THE MANATEE SHORE

The south shore, which falls in Manatee County, has largely been shaped by the Manatee River--a broad, deep flow that offers excellent winter snook fishing in its upper reaches--above the I-75 bridge--in winter. (Don't overlook the Braden River, a smaller flow that joins the Manatee at Ayers Point--it also offers fine topwater plugging in winter.)

The big bridges that span the lower Manatee are also outstanding in summer for snook after dark--drift live shrimp with the current near the pilings. The Green Bridge Fishing Pier, on the north shore at the town of Palmetto, provides

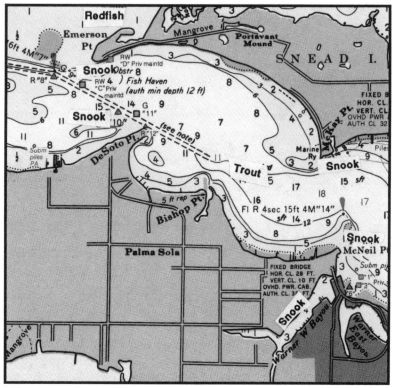

MANATEE RIVER

good action for those without boats, but the U.S. 41 span has more fish if you have a boat to reach them--anchor uptide and drift shrimp or pinfish into the shadows. There's a boat ramp at Riverside Park, on the north side of the river at U.S. 41.

At the mouth of the Manatee River, there's a long sandbar on the north side off Emerson Point. In the summer spawn, loads of snook frequently stack up just off this bar, and can be caught on sardines, pinfish or select shrimp as well as on jigs at times. The drop-off on this bar is a good place to work a small jig for flounder in spring. South of the bar, the river channel opens into a deep hole down to 14 feet, and this is a good spot for spring and fall Spanish mackerel. There's a ramp at Snead Island, on the north side of the river on

The Manatee River has a strong run of snook beginning in November. The fish are often caught at creek mouths on topwater lures.

Snead Island Road in Palmetto, and one on the south side at Warners Bayou Park on North West Riverview Boulevard.

The channel markers are likely to hold cobia in spring, and there are frequently snook and reds in the yellow holes along the shoreline stretching southward to the ICW, the marked navigation channel separating the mainland from Anna Maria Island. The first hundred yards or so of Perico Bayou can also produce snook and reds.

ANNA MARIA

This flat broadens as it approaches Anna Maria, and the outer portions of it, known as The Bulkhead by local anglers,

71

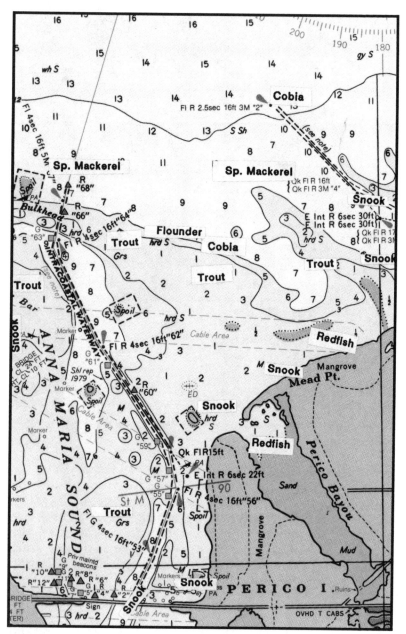

MANATEE RIVER TO ANNA MARIA SOUND

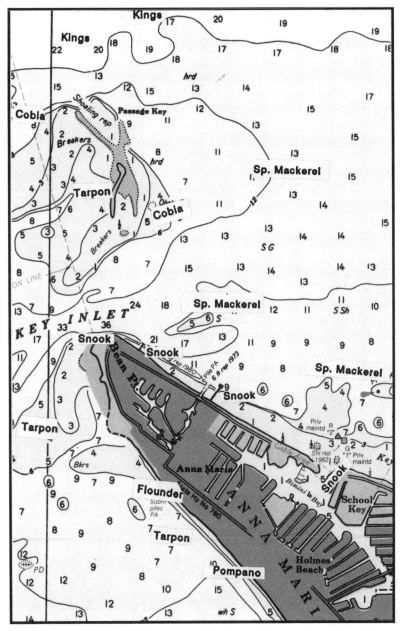

ANNA MARIA AND PASSAGE KEY

has the combination of lush grass and abundant bait that makes ideal seatrout water--fish it on the top third of the tides with topwaters or live sardines. On the late falling tide and the early rise, the outer edge of this flat is good for cobia, flounder and sometimes for schooling reds in late summer and fall. Key Royale Bar and Anna Maria Sound, to the south, are noted areas to net scaled sardines early in the day. It's sometimes worth flipping a few of these along the seawalls at the outlets from Bimini Bay, the access to the Anna Maria harbor, on outgoing tide for snook.

Access to the area is easy from the Kingfish Ramp, on State Route 64 between Perico Island and Anna Maria. Perico Harbor Marina, just east of the ramp, offers tackle and accessories.

THE GULF PASSES

The waters of Passage Key Inlet, which flows around the north tip of Anna Maria, are deep and clear, and hold everything the Gulf has to offer. The two piers here are great night-time snook spots, though you have to go late, be quiet and fish sardines expertly to fool the giants that lay in the lights. By day, these same piers turn out loads of Spanish mackerel from spring through fall.

Walking the beach in summer after dark and casting seaward (your bait is falling into 36 feet of water) with a 65-M MirrOlure or a 1/4 to 1/2 ounce jig head with a Mann's Shadow tail will connect you with whopper snook, as well, and you might stick a hundred-pound tarpon in the same night. Don't wade too deeply in these waters after sundown, however--they're noted for some barrel-chested hammerhead and bull sharks, as well. (If you want to tango with these big boys, put out a whole ladyfish or bonito on 80-pound gear, 12/0 hook and cable leader and dig in your heels.)

By day, the waters of Bean Point, which extends from the tip of Anna Maria seaward, are good places to drift and wait for passing tarpon from May through July. Avoid running your outboard if you try this--the water is clear and the fish are very, very spooky. Captain Paul Hawkins, who is master of the area, says if there are more than a couple of other

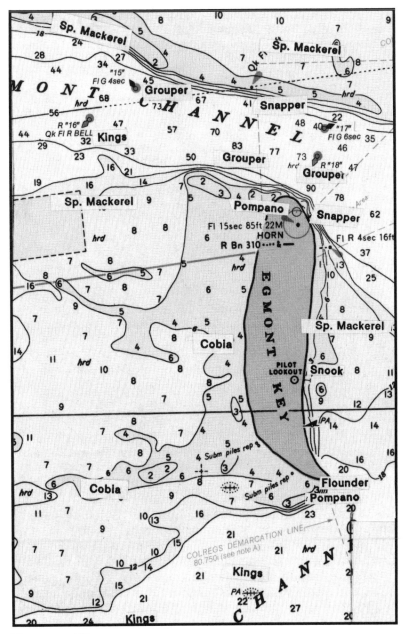

EGMONT KEY

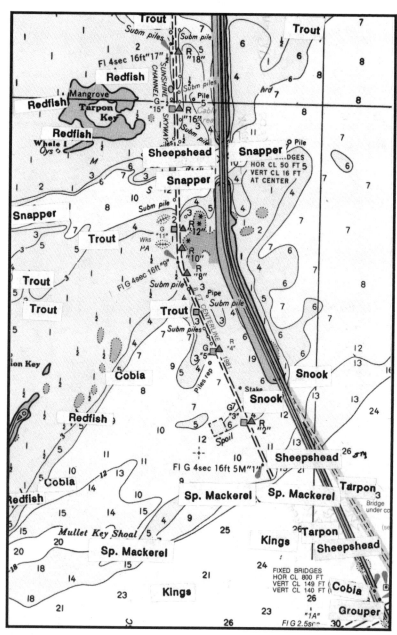

SKYWAY NORTH

76

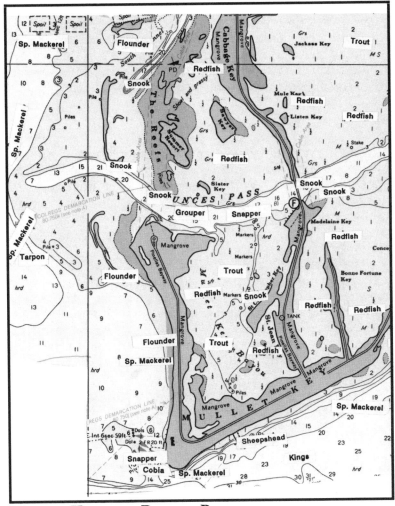

MULLET KEY AND BUNCES PASS

boats on the bar, don't even bother, because the fish won't bite.

The dark-blue channel between Bean Point and Passage Key is good much of the year for Spanish mackerel, and there are frequently cobia poking along the edges of the bar.

The Passage Key Bar occasionally holds tarpon and permit from May through July--but it's a one-boat spot, maybe two, and everybody has to keep their outboards shut off. Even at that, only expert anglers score in the gin-clear water.

Southwest Channel, between Passage and Egmont keys, is a good place to chum with live sardines for Spanish and king mackerel. It used to be a top shark spot, and there are still a few big ones around despite overfishing by the offshore longliners.

EGMONT KEY

The rocks of the old fort on the west shore of Egmont Key sometimes hold big trout in winter, and an occasional cruising cobia on weekdays in summer. The pilot-boat docks on the back side of the island are a noted hangout for giant snook. Forget Egmont on summer weekends, when it's jammed with boats and bikinis--unless you like boats and bikinis, of course.

The Egmont Channel drops vertically into a 90 foot hole just off the north tip of the island, the deepest inshore water anywhere along the west coast, and the rocky ledges hold grouper and snapper if you can ever get a bait near to them in the powerful currents. It's best to fish them on intertidal periods, just at the point the tide starts to move, because when the flow is strong, it's tough to get a bait to the bottom here. It's not a bad idea to put your whitebait down on a wire leader, because you might connect with a big king in the channel as well.

Trolling spoons and small jigs along the long bar that stretches more than three miles seaward from Mullet Key, on the north side of Egmont Channel, frequently turns up Spanish. The channel markers sometimes hold cobia, and those further offshore are good places for smoker kingfish--anchor, chum with snipped threadfins, and free-line live baitfish aft. You'll catch lots of bonita here, as well, maybe more than you want.

THE PINELLAS SHORE

Fort DeSoto State Park on Mullet Key is a delight for anglers, with some of the best boat ramps in the Bay area, plus miles of good beaches, a fully-equipped pier, and lots of

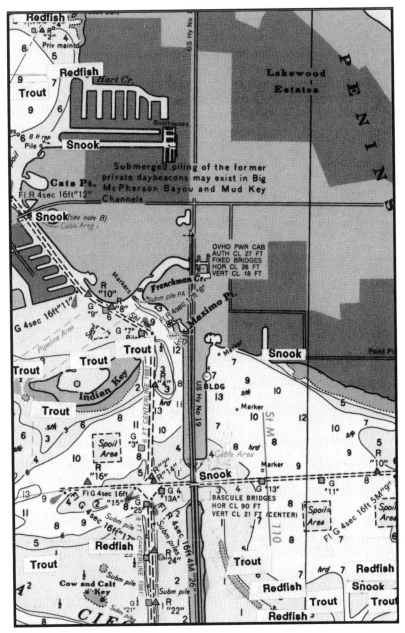

CLAM BAYOU TO MAXIMO POINT

Clear water and shallow flats offer excellent redfish action along the Pinellas County shore. Spoons, topwaters and live sardines are good baits.

flats that can be reached by waders. The water is clear and full of bait from spring through fall, and fishing is usually very good.

The boat ramp is on Bunces Pass, and this cut around the north end of Mullet Key provides good action on trout along its grassy edges, and on snook around the bridges that cross its flow. Tarpon Key, to the northeast, is a good flat to look for reds, while Indian Key, a couple miles north of Tarpon Key, often holds some big trout in the shallow areas near its shores.

The long bar that extends toward the Skyway east from Mullet Key is a good area to drift for trout, and you'll usually find some reds there on rising water. Sand holes produce flounder here. The slightly deeper water beyond the grass is excellent for Spanish mackerel.

There are numerous 2- to 4-foot holes east of Tierra Verde, within a mile of the shore, where trout often gather in summer. The eastern half of this basin is very shallow,

Jumbo snapper like this one caught by Capt. Paul Hawkins are abundant in the ship channels of Tampa Bay. They're usually caught on live sardines fished on the rocky ledges.

averaging a foot on low water, but still holds schools of reds in fall.

Fishing the Skyway reefs or the Mullet Key Channel with a diving plug on a planer or a downrigger will produce pretty good catches of grouper much of the year. Big mangrove snapper scattered along the edge of this channe will bite heavily weighted sardines--sometimes.

CHAPTER 7

SHIVERIN' SHEEPSHEAD

The first thing anybody notices about sheepshead are the teeth. They say the teeth gave them their name. If so, it's a misnomer.

Ever see a sheep that could chew up barnacles, oyster shells and crab chitin like popcorn? Ever see one that could bite right through a fish hook?

Nope, they're nothing like sheep. If sheepshead were mammals, they'd be porcupines.

If they were plants, they'd be cactus.

But they're fish. Some of the spikiest, spiniest fish imaginable. On their ridged backs, they wear a plume of needles that will spear to the bone of any creature--bird, fish or man--brave enough to attempt making them a meal. Similar little daggers arm their pectoral and anal fins, making safe approach from any direction doubtful.

The spines, plus a scaled jacket that could serve as boot leather, make sheepshead low on the list of fish pursued by the majority of anglers. But for those who can overlook the nasty exterior--beauty is only skin deep, remember--

Archosargus probatocephalus is one of the marvels of the Gulf.

Sheepshead are particularly easy to find as winter turns to spring, and a young sheepshead's fancy turns to love. Thousands of them pour into inshore holes and rockpiles to form large spawning aggregations.

The great thing about them, for the boatless fisherman, is that they sometimes stack up in great numbers around certain bridges, piers and rock jetties along our coasts. They like these areas because barnacles also like them, so spend most of their time within range of any angler who would like to drop a line from overhead.

One of the better areas is found at the mouth of Tampa Bay. Here, in March and April, tons of big sheepshead gather around the Sunshine Skyway Bridge and in the adjacent ship channel, providing an outstanding fishery for anglers in the know. Similar gatherings occur like clockwork in many other areas of the Gulf.

Sheepshead look somewhat like overgrown pinfish, sort of plate-shaped and not the least bit likely to be mistaken for sailfish, and so you'd sort of expect them to be piscatorial dummies given to throwing themselves at any bait offered. But, they don't.

In fact, some say the only way to catch sheepshead is to set the hook just before they bite.

'Heads will eat live or freshly-cut shrimp readily, but they will also readily steal it from your hook most of the time if you're not adroit at feeling the bite and reacting.

Experts say the trick is to use a small hook, no larger than a size 1, and bait it with a small chunk of shrimp about the size of your thumbnail. (The hook should be long-shanked. Otherwise, the 'head gets at your leader and nips it off instantly.) This is then sunk straight down beside the piling or rockpile, with just enough weight to sink it in the current. Light tackle helps a lot in feeling the bite--a graphite spinning rig with 10-pound test mono is ideal. Use mono leader if it makes you feel better, but a sheepshead can bite right through even 50-pound-test. On the other hand, you can't use wire because the 'heads will see it. It's probably best to tie direct to the line, in terms of getting more bites.

Sheepshead are powerful fighters and exceptionally tasty on the table. They're abundant throughout Gulf Coast waters, with a strong spawning run inshore in March.

When you make the drop, you keep an eye on the line, and if it stops before it should--before the lead hits bottom-- you take up slack and set the hook.

If it twitches sideways, ditto. And if it seems to be coming right back to the top, set it double quick and double hard. Sheepshead tend to use their sharp, pointed jaws to munch a shrimp off the hook a nibble at a time, but if you use a small chunk and minimal weight, they'll often suck the whole thing in. They don't keep it long, though, because they're used to pulling out the flesh and promptly ejecting the hard left- overs, and that's what they'll do with the hook if you don't act fast.

Some sheepshead experts use light wire hooks, the same sort used for freshwater crappie, so that they can straighten them when the hook snags on the barnacles or oysters. This saves tackle, and the fine wire hooks are easier to sink into a sheepshead's tough mouth.

However, where the 'heads run big, the fine wire may bend out while you're fighting a fish. And occasionally, a fish gets so mad that he can actually chomp right through a fine wire hook and escape.

While shrimp is the easiest bait to obtain and often is effective, sheepshead experts resort to other delicacies to assure their catches. Small fiddler crabs--which can often be found along grassy shorelines or in small mangrove creeks at low tide--are unbeatable. Also outstanding are "tube worms", a creepy saltwater version of the earthworm, found by running a clamming fork or shovel through the mud on flats 1-2 feet deep. Both of these baits seem to have a taste that sheepshead find irresistible, and they'll take them when they completely ignore shrimp.

The one universal in getting sheepshead to bite, whatever the bait, is chumming with their natural food, the barnacle.

The method is simple when fishing a bridge or dock: you simply tie up in an area where the structure is covered with the sharp-shelled mollusks and have at them with any substantial scraper, such as a shovel or garden hoe. Hack, chop and scrape, and you soon send a trail of barnacle puree and broken shells downtide where it rings the dinner bell for any lurking sheepshead. (Redfish, too, if any are close by.)   It usually takes 10 to 15 minutes for the scent message to travel far enough to really get things going. (Choose a piling on the upcurrent side of the structure, so that the scent wafts through all that other likely habitat to pull them in.) Once the fish arrive, they'll be in a feeding mood and readily take your bait.

On open water rockpiles or channels, some anglers carry their chum along, after first knocking the shells off bridges. Crushed oysters also work well.

Sheepshead won't take artificials, in general, though. A sheepshead is not given to pursuing anything that has to be run down, so the darting, swimming action that turns on gamefish to jigs and lures usually does nothing for sheepshead. (Purists can occasionally get one on a 1/8 ounce jig with a brown plastic tail, cut down to about 2 inches long. And-- I haven't tried this but it should work--some fly rod guys tell me they occasionally trick one with an epoxy fly molded to look like a dime-sized crab.)

Sheepshead do get big, incidentally. Though the average catch year around is probably only a couple of pounds, 5-pounders are not uncommon in spring, and I've heard of some that went 8. About 20 years ago, Homosassa guide Gene Lechler got one that weighed over 15 in the Homosassa River in late winter, and the all-tackle IGFA record is 21 pounds, 4 ounces. That fish came from Bayou St. John near New Orleans.

The larger ones are formidable adversaries on light tackle. Picture a five-pound bluegill. They turn that flat side to you and boogie, often right around that barnacle-encrusted piling. Where the fish run large, it's better to go to baitcasting gear and 20-pound test line.

Even with the heavier gear, the only way to win consistently is to get the fish started upward the instant the hook is set. If you carry the strike up high over your shoulder and start cranking instantly, you can often jerk a sheepshead away from a piling before he has time to hunker down. If you're slow, the only thing to do is cuss and tie on a new rig.

In Tampa Bay, the fish gather along the edges of the dredged ship channel, which averages 34 feet deep. It passes through water that averages between 20 and 28 feet, and comes near spoil banks that are less than 15 feet deep. The fish gather in areas where the channel was dredged through rock, or where rock projections have been left near the deep water. It takes a bit of studying the depthfinder, just as if you were grouper fishing, but when you anchor up over the mother lode, every rod in the boat will stay bent as long as you keep a bait in the water.

That's the fun part. They you have to face up to the nasty part, cleaning the pincushions.

Once you've got the beast flopping and gasping on deck your troubles really begin. Best approach is to put the fish on ice as you catch them. This sends them off to sheepshead heaven, and more importantly from your point of view, gets rid of any aggressive tendencies they might show.

You still need a pair of gloves, preferably some of the armored jobs, to protect your hands. Or you might use a pair of poultry shears and snip off the tips of the spines before you start to clean the fish.

Either way, you need a long, thin fillet knife with an extremely sharp edge all the way to the tip. Use the tip to open the skin on either side of the backbone, then slide it right down the spines to separate the filet from the carcass. The extra length of the knife helps keep your hands away from the spines--don't try it with a pocket knife. Get the filets off and away from the carcass, and you're safe.

Then slide the knife between the filet and the skin, cut out the rib cage and you have a slab of snow-white, fine-grained meat that's some of the best the sea has to offer. Dust them with meal and seasonings and fry briefly in smoking peanut oil.

It takes a bit of time and sometimes pain to clean 'heads, and you won't want to clean more than half a dozen or so at a sitting. (A great way to set your boat's limit is to tell each angler they'll be cleaning their own fish.) But the energy required is happily restored when you sit down at the table behind a stack of the filets.

CHAPTER 8

ST. PETERSBURG BEACH TO JOHNS PASS

Though it's one of the most densely developed areas in Florida, the shoreline from St. Petersburg Beach to Clearwater remains highly productive for both inshore and offshore anglers. It's an outstanding area for snook, less so for trout and reds due to minimal grass flats, but the representatives of these latter species found here tend to be big ones. And the offshore waters, thanks to abundant inlets and numerous bottom breaks and valleys, hold excellent fishing for kings and Spanish mackerel. If you're willing to travel well offshore beyond the weekenders, the grouper fishing is very good, as well.

BUNCES PASS

The pass has 20 feet of water running right up to the sand spit on the north end of Mullet Key, and on the unnamed bar on the north side, and both spots can be good in summer for lunker snook on falling tides. The point where the deep water fades out into the bars at the mouth of the pass also hold fish in summer, but this is mostly a night-time spot

Cobia prowl the coast from March through October, often hanging around offshore channel markers. They take large jigs, jumbo shrimp and live baitfish.

because boat traffic spooks the fish by day. Of course, winds must be calm or from the east, or breakers make the area unfishable. Live sardines, select shrimp or 1/2 ounce jigs with 4-inch shad-type plastic tails do the job. There are some whopper flounder in this same area in spring.

The water drops from 4 feet on the Bunces Pass Bar to 14 feet just beyond, and you can often find mackerel by trolling the edge of this drop with silver spoons. Tarpon occasionally show up in the basin on the south end of Mullet Key, moving out of the depths of Egmont Channel, mostly June through July.

The ruins of the old pier on the southwest tip of Mullet Key sometimes hold snook--it's mostly a night spot for topwater plugging, June through August.

PASS A GRILLE

The inside waters of Pass A Grille Channel are broad and deep, up to 42 feet in some spots, and form a natural winter

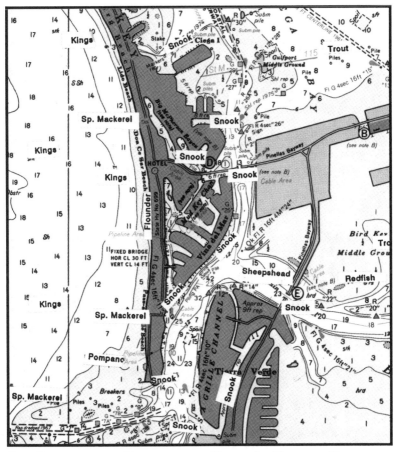

ST. PETERSBURG BEACH AND PASS A GRILLE CHANNEL

basin for all sorts of critters, including some broadshouldered snook, big trout and reds, sheepshead and even grouper.

All the docks on the main pass, beginning around Marker 11, are likely for snook. These docks stand in about 10 feet and it's only a few yards to 20-foot depths, plus there's continual current flow; the sort of area big linesiders love. The fish bite best from November through February around those docks with powerful lights--you can usually see them lying there like gray logs.

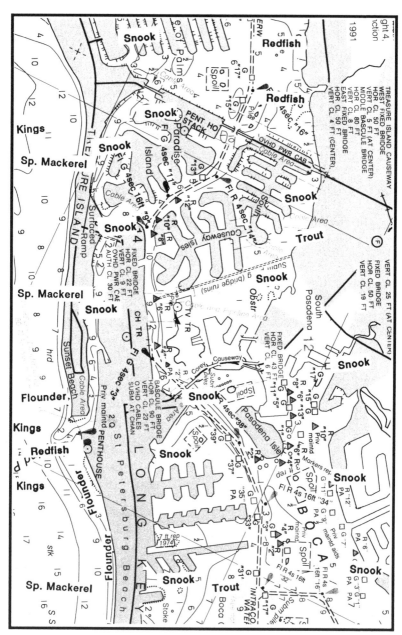

TREASURE ISLAND AND BLIND PASS

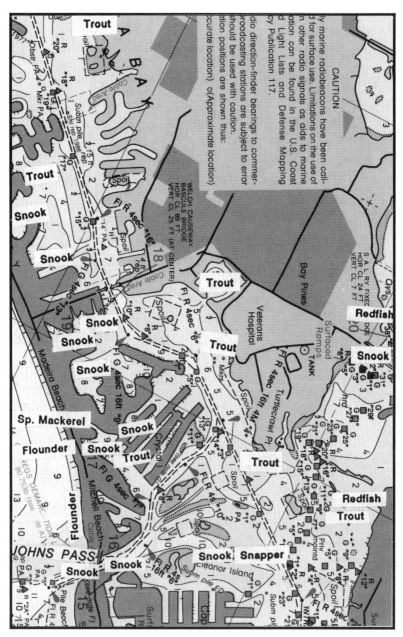

MADEIRA BEACH AND JOHN'S PASS

93

Snook are frequent catches on the grassy flats on both sides of Bunces Pass. Topwater plugs make for exciting strikes.

King mackerel are abundant in April and again in October and November, but some fish hang around all summer. Spoons trolled on a planer are the most dependable producers, but for lunkers, live sardines or threadfins are hard to beat.

The trick is to stay well back from the lighted areas and cast unweighted shrimp, baitfish or small jigs or streamer flies to them. Often, casts to the outer perimeter of the lighted areas draw the hits, while those in the bright areas with visible fish are ignored.

You'll see a lot more fish than you'll catch, but if you're quiet and happen to be there at the right time--most likely on a strong outgoing tide--you'll see snook pandemonium. (Don't plan a trip on the main channel when there's a strong winter wind out of the north--it gets rough, making for miserable boat handling, and the fish are hard to see in the chop.)

There are dozens of side canals making off the main channel, both into Tierra Verde on the east and St. Petersburg Beach on the west, and all of these are possibles for snook as well as seatrout in winter. Use an electric trolling motor to ease along the canals after dark and you'll find endless fishing opportunities. Some of the well-to-do home owners may fuss at you for invading their back yards, but it's public water and they can't toss you out. Just don't step on their docks or hook their docklines.

The South Pass A Grille Channel, which runs south to nowhere these days, dead-ending in the flats west of Cabbage Key, has depths of up to 20 feet and sometimes gets runs of trout on the first cold snaps of winter. It's also possible snook water, with the best area likely to be the point where it joins the North Channel. The edges of this channel frequently hold nice flounder spring through fall.

The last docks on North Channel, at the tip of Pass A Grille Beach, are noted as holding spots for monster snook-- and we're talking fish in excess of 30 pounds--from May through July. Big live mullet or ladyfish are the preferred baits, and 50-pound gear, minimum, if you want to get one to the boat. St. Pete Beach Boat Ramp, off East 33rd Avenue, is a handy place to launch for all of the above.

There's good fishing for lunker-sized king mackerel in April and again in November from the North Channel marker 2 northward to Johns Pass, anywhere from 100 yards off the beach on out to 25-foot depths. It's here where famed king-fish angler and conservationist Gene Turner made many of his most impressive catches.

The Don CeSar Hotel is a good landmark to start your day--it sits due east from a nipple of 17-foot water that juts into deeper water on both sides, and often holds lots of threadfins for bait as well as the kings that eat them. Most lunkers are caught by anchoring, chumming with cut thread-fins, and free-lining live ones on 4/0 hooks and a short length of single-strand wire.

The aptly named Blind Pass, which cuts off Treasure Island from Long Key, is almost invisible from seaward be-cause it makes a 90-degree dogleg just after clearing the beach. But the inside waters have depths of 9 feet or so, and lots of docks that hold winter trout, reds and snook. Pass under the bridge and around the tip of Long Key and you come into dozens of residential finger channels lined with docks that occasionally hold fish. In general, those with biggest snook are on canals with tide flowing through, rather than the ones that dead-end. Trout, on the other hand, are where you find them--inspect every lighted dock you see.

CHAPTER 9

CLEARWATER AND ST. JOSEPH SOUND

The inside waters from Johns Pass northward to The Narrows, where the ICW runs through a narrow neck of water, are all good snook country. The fish hang around the lighted docks pretty much year around, providing excellent action after dark. In winter, they're sometimes joined by schools of spotted seatrout and some jumbo redfish.

One of the better areas for both snook and reds in the larger sizes is the Johns Pass Bridge. The area gets lots of heat early in the evening from shore anglers, but after midnight things calm down and the fish start to bite under the lights on both the inside and outside. Live pinfish dropped to bottom are often a good bet--use heavy tackle, because the fish run 10 pounds and up.

There are finger channels due east of the pass where cuts of 10 to 15 feet split the flats. The edges of these shoal areas are often good at dawn for snook and for jumbo trout. The flats to the east of the Long Bayou Channel also hold nice trout at times, in water as shallow as 18 inches. Johns Pass Marina has ramps, bait, ice, etc.--it's on Kingfish Drive.

Following the ICW north from the pass you progress into the Redington Beach area, which has a lot of 8-foot deep water around residential docks. These are all possible snook spots in summer, and often hold snook, trout and reds in winter. On rising water, you can sometimes catch all three species on some of the narrow flats that extend away from these deeper dredged areas in this northernmost extreme of Boca Ciega Bay. War Veterans Memorial Park, off Alternate 19 in Seminole, provides boat ramps, as does Madeira Beach Municipal Marina, off 150th Avenue in Madeira Beach.

INDIAN ROCKS BEACH

There's a unique topography to the gulf bottom off Indian Rocks Beach, with ragged shoals extending westward for several miles. On the tip of the shoal, you're four miles from the beach and still in only 15 feet of water, while the water on either side is 20 to 25 feet deep.

The coastline makes an elbow to the west here, which creates the erratic bottom, and the structure attracts bait, which attracts migrating kings, mackerel, bonito, cobia and so on. The breaks and fingers repeat themselves around the 30-foot contour, where you'll find abrupt drops to 40 feet. The result is tide rips, surfacing bait, diving birds--and gamefish.

CLEARWATER HARBOR

North of Bellaire Causeway, Clearwater Harbor opens into a broad and fairly deep sound, with depths of 5 to 7 feet common. There's a 16-foot deep dredge-hole north of Howard Point where trout sometimes stack up in cold weather, and you may catch some big snapper and sheepshead in there on live shrimp, as well.

The spoil islands west of the ICW sometimes hold nice trout spring through fall--fish topwater plugs in areas with lots of mullet showing. Wading will get more fish than staying in the boat in these clear areas. Indian Rocks Ramp, on 3rd Avenue off Gulf Boulevard, is close-by.

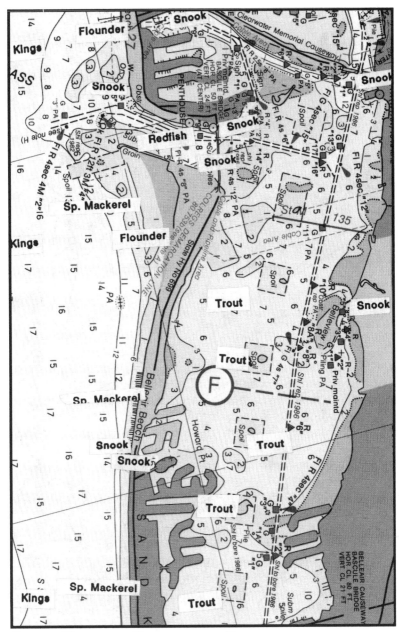

SAND KEY AND CLEARWATER PASS

The offshore waters near Clearwater Pass have been one of the hottest locations for king mackerel in recent years. Fish are found anywhere from 100 yards off the beach to 20 miles out.

CLEARWATER

The south jetty at Clearwater Pass is a noted gathering spot for oversized redfish in fall and early winter, and also holds big snook all summer long. Snook also prowl the beaches at Belleair Beach and Clearwater Beach, particularly in the areas where groins have been placed to prevent erosion. Fish these locations early on summer mornings with topwaters or live sardines.

The back side of the harbor, due east of the pass, has shallow flats breaking off the ICW where you might run into a bit of anything on the last half of rising tides--snook, reds, trout and even the occasional cobia show up here thanks to the deep water channel cut directly in from the gulf.

The ICW opens into a 14-foot deep hole just north of the Clearwater Causeway, and this can be a winter-time assembly point for schools of trout.

Mandalay Channel, which runs along the east shore of Clearwater Beach, has some deep water under the docks, and often holds summer snook. The fish sometimes work their

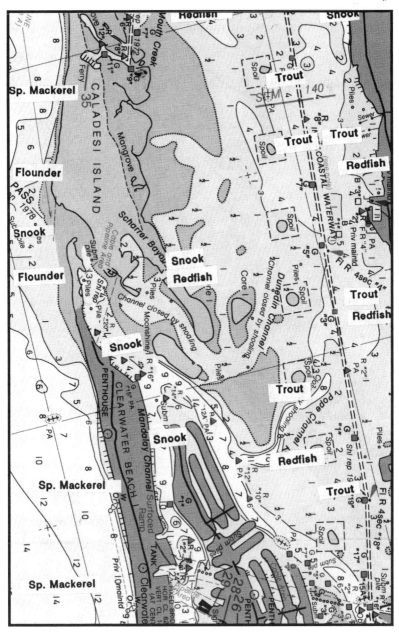

CLEARWATER BEACH AND CALADESI ISLAND

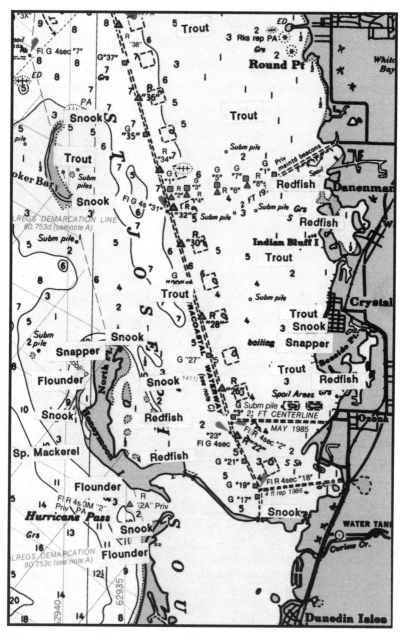

HONEYMOON ISLAND AND THREE ROOKER BAR

Many summer snook are jumbos, but all must be released due to the closed season June through August. Wade-fishermen often score best due to their low profile.

way pretty well back toward what used to be Dunedin Pass-- ease along on a trolling motor casting as close to the cover as possible.

There's a dredge hole along the east short of the harbor at Dunedin Isles, with 10 feet of water right against shore-- always a low-tide possible for snook, and a "maybe" spot for winter trout and reds.

Belleair Beach Causeway ramp, off State Road 686, is a good place to launch.

HONEYMOON ISLAND

Hurricane Pass, on the south end of Honeymoon Island, is too shallow to hold spawning snook, but there's a 10-foot hole just outside the pass at Marker 2A that's worth probing on summer mornings before the water gets rough. There are occasionally some tarpon hanging around this area in June and July, as well.

North Point, on Honeymoon's north end, is a famed summer snook spot. It has a unique bottom structure, with a

Snook jam the smaller passes in summer as they gather for their spawn. Jigs or live bait bounced along bottom on strong tide flows result in fast action when the fish are in.

deep but narrow cut running around the point. Depths here are 10 to 12 feet, and the fish may be anywhere from the gulf side to east of Grassy Key. They take live sardines, 1/2 ounce jigs and sinking plugs, with action hottest on outgoing tides. The fish run big here, with 8 pounds average, 15 to 20 not rare.

On the back side of Honeymoon, St. Joseph Sound opens up to its maximum two-mile width, with a whole lot of water in the 4- to 6-foot range bottomed with grass--excellent trout water so long as there's reasonable water clarity. Some of the area is bare sand, however--move until you find the grass patches.

Numerous spoil islands are east of the ICW here. The water is pretty murky due to boat traffic on weekends, but on weekday mornings and evenings there are sometimes some large trout in close to these shoals. Fish a noisy topwater where you see bait schooling in water 1 to 3 feet deep. (Yep, the big guys are up there in the shallows. Smaller school trout are more common in water 4 to 7 feet deep.)

Sutherland Bayou, just north of the Ozona Channel, is sometimes worth poling into on high water--snook settle into the deep holes in the back section at times.

There's a 14-foot hole off Seaside Point in this area, surrounded by 2-foot depths. It can be a good low tide spot, but you might have to push your boat to get there in winter.

Both the north and south points of Three Rooker Bar, just north of Honeymoon, are good summer snook spots. The place is jammed with boaters on weekends, but usually has little traffic weekdays. Stand on the points, cast uptide and let the current bring your lure back down, just tickling bottom.

There are some grass patches in the little flat on the back side where you can sometimes pop up enough trout for supper, after you're done wrestling with the snook. Access to all of these waters is easy via fish camp ramps in Ozona.

CHAPTER 10

ANCLOTE KEYS

The Anclote Keys are beautiful, unspoiled, and surrounded by fish much of the year. The area is the starting point for the broad, shallow grass flats that stretch northward for more than a hundred miles, and is thus a natural for all sorts of gamefish. It also sits just off the mouth of the Anclote River, a fertile estuary that makes the angling here even better.

THE KEYS

There are actually seven islands in the Anclote Keys, plus several very shallow bars on the north and south ends that could readily become islands themselves with the help of a few mangrove shoots. But, there's also really deep water cutting around both the north and south tips of the main island, Anclote Key, and this creates a snook fishery that has to be seen to be believed in June, July and August.

The south tip has 13 feet coming right against the beach, the north end as much as 18 feet. On the north side there's actually a double channel separated by a bar about 3 feet

The sandy points of the Anclote Keys are good areas to fish for snook, pompano and a bit of everything else. Deep water passes close to shore, creating a fish highway within casting range of waders.

deep, and both these channels sometimes hold fish. Action is usually best on falling tide.

The cuts may also hold a lot of other stuff, ranging from trout to cobia to mackerel to the occasional tarpon and whopper sharks. Fish the edge of the drop and you'll catch flounder except in the dead of winter. Tons of bait passes in and out on the tides, and this creates a natural feeding area for game species.

The beach gets busy on weekends, but on weekdays there are few boats, and sometimes in summer you'll encounter large pods of snook lazing along anywhere from 20 feet off the sand on out. Run the edge looking for fish, or walk the length and cast ahead at dawn--a nice outing.

The back side of the island is mangroves leading into a very shallow flat, but on high water there's enough depth to pole and sometimes you'll find both reds and snook prowling there. (Very spooky fish, though, usually requiring long casts with live sardines to get them. Captain Mike DuClon is among the masters of this area.)

Cobia sometimes cruise along within a hundred yards of the beach, as well as over the north and south bars, so it pays

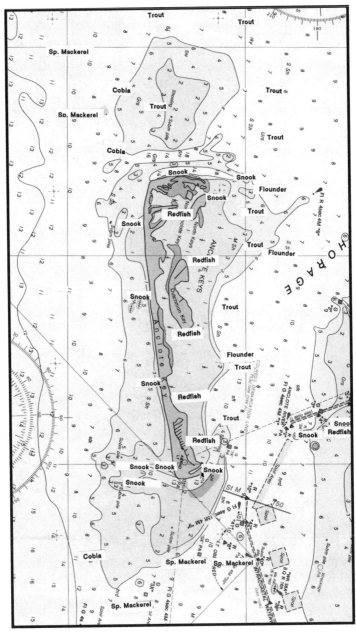

THE ANCLOTE KEYS

The Anclote River has prime winter fishing for snook. Live sardines and topwater plugs are best.

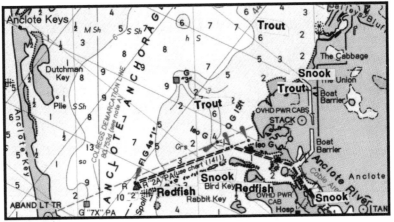

ANCLOTE RIVER

to keep your eyes open for the big brown shadows. Off the south bar, there are Spanish mackerel pretty much year around, though they get scarce after big cold fronts in late December and on through February. Most guys get them by trolling a chrome spoon on a small planer.

Off the north end, grass flats grow out as deep as 12 feet, and you may find schools of trout anywhere from the outer edge of this grass all the way back to the shoreline. In general, the fish are deeper in summer, shallower in spring and fall.

You'll see a lot of boats fishing right around Marker 4, north of the island, but they're there mostly because it's a fixed location easy to find. The larger schools of trout are usually anywhere from 1 to 5 miles north of this marker, usually in slight depressions where the surrounding water is about 8 feet deep.

Best bait for these fish is usually a 1/8 to 1/4 ounce jig with a shad-type tail, fished right along bottom. Cast ahead of the boat as you drift, but slip the anchor if you catch several in succession.

It's not a bad idea to toss out a noisy topwater like the Spook or 5M MirrOlure on occasion. Though this is deeper water than normal for topwaters, nice catches of large trout are sometimes made with this method. Apparently the fish can see the bait a considerable distance in the clear water.

The outer edge of this broad grass prairie, known as "salt and pepper" bottom by locals because of the mottled appearance, is an excellent spot for Spanish mackerel. Anchor right on the break on incoming tides and put out a chum bag of ground fish or sardines in oil. Limit catches usually come in short order, either on fast-moving jigs and spoons or on live sardines. The outer edge nearest the north bar is noted for producing Spanish over 5 pounds with some regularity.

ANCLOTE ANCHORAGE

The bay that separates the keys from the mainland is Anclote Anchorage, about 3 miles wide and averaging about 6 to 7 feet deep. The water is often murky due to boat traffic, but when it clears it's good trout water. The east edges, where the depths shoal to 3 feet, are grassy and usually hold scattered trout--good topwater area. As you approach the shoreline, in water about 2 feet deep, you enter redfish water. There are not the dense populations here you see in larger bays, but persistent sight fishing will result in a good number of opportunities in a day.

The spoil bars south of the main Anclote River Channel have holes and cuts between them, and these often hold snook, reds and trout, best caught on live sardines or live shrimp from a boat anchored at maximum casting range.

The north channel of the Anclote, which veers out of the main channel at Marker 8, is a good low tide spot for reds, trout, drum and whatever happens to be swimming on the 2-foot-deep flats on either side. The channel averages 7 feet deep. Give it a visit when a big spring tide is drawing everything off the shallow areas adjacent, fishing jigs in the middle, topwaters off the edges, or live sardines most anywhere.

The warm water outflow of the Tarpon Springs electrical power plant about a mile north of the river holds all sorts of fish all winter. Fishing is best after dark on frosty nights with live shrimp drifted just off bottom--many jumbo trout are taken this way, and there are also runs of small permit in the area at times, best caught on small fiddler crabs.

Launch areas on the lower Anclote include Duke's Fish Camp, plus a large public park just downriver.

THE ANCLOTE RIVER

As you enter the river, redfish often prowl the rising water near a couple of spoil bars south of Marker 16.

The entire lower end of the Anclote River, including Spring Bayou and Kreamer Bayou, have scattered snook around the docks in spring, summer and fall. Boat traffic makes fishing tough by day, but if you ease into these areas at night and make accurate casts close to the pilings, you'll find good action.

In winter, a good number of the snook head upriver beyond the Alternate 19 bridge. This is a pretty saltmarsh basin with little human habitation until you get far up stream, and fishing can be hot from December through early March. However, the water is very shallow between holes and the bottom is limerock in many areas--go slowly and cautiously if you value your lower unit, or hire a guide who knows the area--Dave Markett is one of the best here. The fish usually hit best over the holes on low tide, and at creek mouths on the fall. Topwaters are the best offering.

NORTH OF THE ANCLOTE

The flat between the two channels that lead into Gulf Harbors sometimes holds reds and trout--topwaters or weedless spoons are the ticket. Visit the mouths of the main canals in Gulf Harbors on falling water at dusk for some impressive snook.

The large park at the mouth of the river, reached off Anclote Boulevard from Alternate 19, is the spot where most folks launch, but it's a zoo on weekends, usually involving a wait in line. Duke's Fish Camp, just before you get to the park, is a lot quieter and offers ice, bait and free advice. There's an up-river ramp at Craig Park, off Spring Boulevard in Tarpon Springs, and one on St. Joseph Sound at Sunset Beach Park, on Gulf Road.

CHAPTER 11

LOOK OUT, OLD MACK IS BACK!

Mack the knife is back.

Gulf Coast anglers have been covered up with the best mackerel runs in decades the last few years, and things look even better for the future thanks to strict harvest regulations.

The fish are not only along the beaches, where they're supposed to be, but are running far up into the larger bays where they haven't been seen in years. Anglers in the Tampa Bay area report lots of fish at Gandy Bridge and Courtney Campbell Causeway, many miles from the open Gulf, and the voracious speedsters even showed up well inside brackish rivers including the Manatee and Little Manatee in recent seasons.

The most remarkable aspect of the action is that it is so widespread, indicating not simply one large school migrating through, but a very large number of fish spread over a very large area. The distance from Sanibel to Cedar Key is some 200 miles, and anglers at every port along the way but recent spring runs have bent rods throughout the whole area from March through early May. For anyone who loves mackerel fishing, this is a time to re-discover this sleek speedster, and enjoy action like the good old days.

MACKEREL TACKLE

Mackerel are among the fastest fish in the sea, but in order to strut their stuff they have to have a light drag to work against. Best choice, therefore, is a light-action, 7-foot spinning rod, an open-faced reel with a smooth drag lightly set, and a full charge of 6-pound or 8-pound test mono.

Matched against this gear, you can expect a hooked Spanish to deliver some smoking, reel-screeching runs--and the big ones will show you the spool at times.

Mackerel are toothy critters, and you have to have a leader of some sort to protect your light line from their choppers. Best, most experts agree, is 30-pound-test mono, because this is clear enough and fine enough that the fish can't see it. Fine wire also works, but you'll get twice the strikes on mono, and only occasionally does a fish chop it off. (Of course, if you're fishing where Spanish and kings mix, as they often do, go with the wire because the stronger bite of a king almost always parts the mono.)

Most pros also avoid using swivels, because mackerel are notorious for homing in on them and chopping off the running line behind. The exception is when you're towing a spoon, which twists the line without the swivel.

BAITS AND LURES

When mackerel are hot, driving bait on top and foaming up acres of water under diving gulls, you'd swear that anything that hits the water would catch them.

Not so, however.

They can be maddeningly selective at times, and are particularly partial to tiny offerings when they feed on the inch-long silver darts known as "glass minnows". If you hit a school bent on the tiny baits, it's best to break out the fly rod and offer them a tiny glass-minnow streamer, basically a nearly-bare hook with the shank wrapped in silver and just a

Spanish mackerel, in short supply in the mid-1980's due to overfishing, are again abundant throughout west coast waters. The strongest runs are in March and April, and again in October and November, but the growing population has offered good fishing all summer in recent years.

twist of hair aft. Small jigs, 1/8 ounce heads and tails about 2 inches long, and similarly small chrome spoons also get them when they're chasing minnows.

At other times, mackerel truly go nuts and really will grab anything--jigs, spoons, sinking plugs or floaters--so long as it moves FAST!

Mackerel, more than any other species, are triggered into striking by a bait or lure that seems to be running away from them. If it slows down, they don't want it.

So, the trick is to make long casts and get the lure coming back to you very fast, with long whips of the rod and vigorous cranking of the reel. Reels with high gear ratios, 5:1 and up, help a lot.

In trolling, the lure also needs to move right along, 5 to 7 knots. If you go slow, you'll catch some, but the fast lures usually outfish the slow ones considerably.

For big fish, the chrome Rat-L-Trap cranked hard is particularly effective. Other plugs that get them include the 38M MirrOlure and the Rattlin' Flash. Mackerel also hit topwaters very well, though few anglers try them. Among the better lures are the 28 M MirrOlure and the Bangolure SP-5. Work them fast, loud and splashy, and hang on tight--a mackerel strike on top is something to see.

Top live baits are scaled sardines, netted on inside grass flats, and threadfins or "greenbacks", which can be netted along the beaches or caught by dangling #10 gold hooks off the piers.

These baits can be used as chum by snipping them up with bait shears, or they can be bounced off the outboard to go wobbling downtide as live chum. The latter method often works best for bringing in really big Spanish, and is likely to lure up a smoker-sized king mackerel, as well.

The sardines are fished unweighted, on 1/0 hooks threaded through the tough spot above the nose.

When sardines are tough to find, live shrimp also work well, especially if you chop some up to lead mackerel to the whole ones on your hook.

Ground, frozen chum blocks available at fish houses are prime chum, as well. Hang it in a mesh bag off the transom. Canned, fish-flavor catfood also makes a good mackerel chum at times.

WHERE TO FIND A BIG MACK

The Tampa Bay area has produced some of the biggest mackerel on record, including the 8-pound, 7-ounce IGFA 4-pound test record taken by James Wisner in 1985 and the 5-pound, 5-ounce women's 4-pound record taken by Bonnie Powell in 1986.

The all-tackle record, a 12-pound monster, was taken off Ft. Pierce in 1984. (You'd never guess where the runner-up was taken, however: the 10-pound, 15-ounce giant was caught at Oak Bluffs, Massachusetts!)

Specifically, mackerel tend to gather in areas of strong tide flow created by causeways, spoil islands and bars. Thus, the Sunshine Skyway is always a good place to start--and the long piers there make great fishing for shorebound anglers.

Also good are the bars on the south side of the main ship channel leading from the Skyway east and north. Locations where side channels meet the main channel are often good, as well. The idea is to find an area where water 15 to 20 feet deep pushes up against a shoal 8 to 10 feet deep. This creates a good ambush area for the mackerel, and the swirling water usually holds bait, so such locations are always worth a few casts.

The edges of the bars along the Egmont Channel are always productive, and anglers on the piers at Fort DeSoto catch their share at this time of year.

In fact, nearly each pass that meets the Gulf creates a bar jutting off the beach, and there are usually mackerel somewhere close by.

At Cedar Key, Seahorse Reef juts far offshore, and is an absolutely killer spot for big macks as well as kings. St. Martin's Reef off Hudson is similarly productive.

Off Crystal River, Homosassa and south to Anclote Key, the areas where the grass flats meet the bare sand of the open Gulf, in depths from 8 to 14 feet, are very dependable.

Mackerel can also be found at random in many areas in between those mentioned, sometimes right in the wash of the surf, sometimes 15 or 20 miles out. These roaming fish are usually located by looking for diving birds or breaking bait.

You can also simply put a small jig or spoon behind the boat 150 feet or so and pull until you get a bite. If you sink it down on a small planer, the bites will come more quickly.

The only secret to catching mackerel these days is to keep moving until you hit the schools--you'll know it immediately when you're in the right spot. (Look for clear water, or the edge where clear water meets murky water--mackerel won't hit in cloudy water, but they love that edge.)

The action usually gets going strong around mid-March, and continues through April. There's a slow-down in mid-summer, and then another big push from mid-October through Thanksgiving. In mild winters, fishing remains good straight on through to spring.

Mackerel are not good fish for catch-and-release unless you use single hook rigs. Fish that are handled for more than a minute or two don't usually survive release, so you have to be quick. It's a good idea to use barbless hooks and long-nose pliers and simply shake the fish off in the water. You'll lose a few due to the absent barbs, but it won't matter much. Old Mack is finally back, and if one gets away, another won't be long in taking hold.

CHAPTER 12

PITHLACHASCOTEE TO WEEKI WACHEE

Below our feet, a shag carpet of yellow and green and brown unrolls as we slide along on a glass-smooth tide. In the saltmarsh, a rail calls, the only interruption in the silence except for the solid "thwack" of mullet, falling like dropped ballbats, back into the warm bay.

"Hit the points," suggests Captain Dennis Royston, leaning on the control of the trolling motor. "Early tide like this, they'll be there."

The rods whicker in the still air, whipping silvery plastic torpedoes to fall gently at the edge of the needlerush. We begin the game, the lures jumping up on top, skirting and skimming back and forth, can't make up their mind, in the mad dance of dying bait.

Nothing on the first point. Nothing, either, on the second. Throats cleared, impatience, faith failing--until the lure dances across the third point and disappears in a sudden implosion, as though a cement block has fallen on the surface and pulled the bait down after it.

Snook are found in good numbers as far north as Hudson, but are rare further north due to their tropical nature. Most are caught in creek mouths and bays in summer, and in residential canals in winter.

The rod creaks under the weight of the fish, and the reel begins to slip, just a bit at first, then a rising siren song. The snook shoves a big, green head through the glass calm, wallows, spits water, flexes his shoulders, then turns and heads for the marsh.

Royston hustles the boat between the fish and the shoreline, heads him off and herds him back to the open water, and five minutes later the yard-long slab of silver stretches across the front deck, the yellow fins catching the early sun. Photos, revival, release--and another big fish on the next point, and then on the next.

We saw not another boat the whole morning, except for the distant passing of a commercial fisherman seeking mullet. The Hudson area is major habitat break on the gulf shoreline, the point at which the white sand beaches further south convert to broad, shallow grass flats, and like such habitat breaks in most areas, it's a fertile fishery. The shoreline is low-lying saltmarsh, undeveloped and undevelopable,

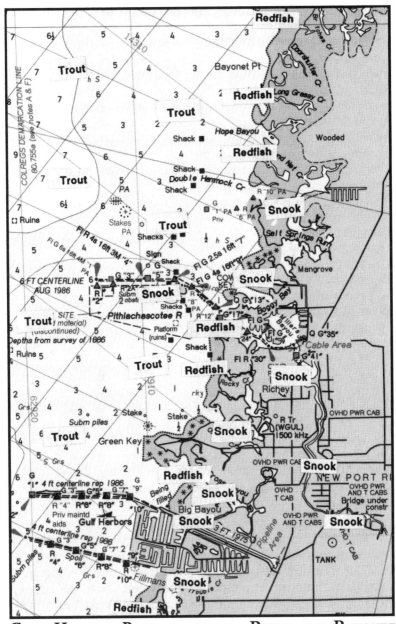

GULF HARBOR, PITHLACHASCOTEE RIVER AND BAYONET POINT

giving the estuaries a pristine solitude that's rare in the Florida of the 1990's.

Anglers have worked the outer edges of the grass for decades for trout and Spanish mackerel, but until recent seasons, few realized that many of the best fishing opportunities were behind them when they got beyond the last channel marker. It's roughly 40 miles from Anclote to Chassahowitzka Point, just south of Homosassa Bay, and the shoreline and its myriad creeks and bays in all of that distance provides outstanding opportunities for sightfishing redfish. In the southern half, snook are large and abundant. And each of the deeper bays has good seatrout populations, with bonus shots at torpedo-sized cobia spring through fall.

The reason the area has been largely left alone is the stone-hard bottom, which is completely unforgiving for anglers who underestimate their draft. Unlike most other areas around the Gulf Coast where you can guess at the depth and depend on a stainless prop to make up the difference as it buzzes through mud or soft sand, much of this area has a limerock base which is murder on skegs and props. The hard bottom and the lack of major freshwater rivers keeps the water crystal clear, but the price of lower units has kept most would-be flats anglers at bay.

However, for the few who probe the area, the rewards are considerable. The water is clearer than anywhere else outside the Florida Keys, and visually locating snook and reds at distances of a hundred yards or more is a daily happening. Cobia are bonus fish in spring, summer and fall, as they cruise the bays in singles and pairs, or often in whole schools plowing along in the wake of a big ray. Presenting a topwater or a flyrod streamer to a 40-pounder in waist-deep water is an experience not to be missed.

NORTHERNMOST SNOOK

On the morning of our trip, in late May, we saw more than 30 snook podded on the grass points and along mangrove shorelines. The area is at the northern end of snook range, but warm winters the past three years have created an abundant population, with lots of fish in the 7- to 15-pound range.

The waters between Hudson and Aripeka are rimmed with salt marsh, and the outer edges of these broad, grassy areas are good for both snook and reds on high tides.

Best snook action is roughly from the fishing village of Aripeka southward.

Reds are found throughout the area, with especially good fishing from June through November as schools of bronze bombers in the 10- to 15-pound range cruise the oyster bars and the edges of the marsh looking for crabs, shrimp and finger mullet. Seatrout fishing is best in late March, April and May, as spawners move onto the flats, and again in November as the fish feed heavily before the first fronts.

For snook, best lures are mullet imitations, with the hot offering currently a soft-plastic, bullet-shaped bait known as the "Reel Magic". The lure weighs half an ounce and allows for the long casts necessary for effectively fishing the clear shallows, yet it's light enough to dance on the surface when you walk-the-dog with rapid twitches of the rod. It's also weedless, especially important here since there's inevitably lots of loose, floating grass around the better points when the tide is flowing strongly. Best colors, local anglers say, are the silver flake and gold flake, and a pearly hue known as "rainbow trout".

The bait is danced along until it draws a strike, then the rod is dropped, slack taken up and the hook set, much as in fishing a plastic worm for bass. Fish usually hang on to the soft plastic body, allowing plenty of time to drive the hook home.

Other good lures include the MirrOlure 7M and 28 M and the Bangolure SP-5 among floaters, and the 52 M MirrOlure and the Rattlin' Flash among slow-sinkers. The Slug-Go and the Jerk Worm, longer soft-plastics, also do well fished unweighted on 5/0 hooks. Small, plastic-tailed jigs are effective, and for the redfish, the traditional weedless spoon in gold finish is hard to beat.

The bite is usually on the outside points at the first of the rising tide, moving to inside bays and points as the tide progresses. On the fall, channels between oyster bars and at creek mouths are usually good. Trout are caught over the grass in the larger bays on either tide, whenever the water is moving well.

Here's a closer look at some specific hotspots:

THE PITHLACHASCOTEE RIVER

The 'Cotee, as it's known locally, is home to Steve Marusak, who heads Cotee Jigs, and in winter Marusak never leaves the river to load up on leg-long snook. The fish go all the way to the head of navigable water, and feed best on the high falling tide at creek mouths, in the deep bends and corners on low water. Marusak likes jigs, of course, but topwaters work well in the upper river, deep diving crank baits and select shrimp in the holes.

There are numerous rocky bars in the lower river, beginning just west of the public park and boat ramp at the U.S. 19 bridge. (The park is about 300 yards from the highway, a right and then a left turn. The trailer space fills early on weekends.) These bars, usually ignored by people in a hurry to get offshore, are excellent redfish spots on rising water in fall. Go around the corner to the south into Rocky Creek or Oyster Creek, or to the north to Boggy Bay or Double Hammock Creek. This is poling or wading water, not planing water, and you'll want to go on the last half of the rise and the first hour of the fall. Topwaters in this area will often catch snook and redfish, but the tight confines and shallows make the fish very sensitive to motion and boat noise.

Rich grass flats extend almost all the way to shore here, and run westward for more than 8 miles, out to depths of 14 feet. The area looks like trout heaven, and it frequently is. There was a down cycle in the area the last few years, but the past summer the fish appeared once again, and anglers fishing jigs on bottom regularly catch 30 to 50 per day. The fish tend to congregate in areas of "broken" bottom, with scattered sand patches. They also rise to hit topwaters, even in water as deep as 10 feet, and the ones that come up are usually keepers. The deeper grass is best in summer, while in spring and fall the fish move within a mile or two of shore in water 3 to 5 feet deep.

In the summer, snook sometimes gather around spoil islands along the south side of the main river channel as it passes across the flats. You may also catch reds close to the rockpiles, and trout water begins just south of them.

THE ST. MARTINS REEFS

South St. Martins Reef is about 3 miles northwest of the last channel marker on the Pithlachascotee channel--it's frequently a good spot for big trout and Spanish mackerel.

Continue another 6 miles northwest to St. Martins Reef proper, which is marked by a flashing marker. The shoal itself is about a mile southeast of the marker--it rises to 5 feet in surrounding depths of 12 to 13 feet, and is a surefire spot for Spanish from April through November. Kings often gather in great schools just west of the marker, where they can be chummed in with cut sardines or caught by trolling spoons or jigs on a planer.

You'll even find the occasional lunker barracuda hanging around these offshore markers in late summer, but they disappear as soon as the water begins to cool in October. Live baitfish or tube lures pulled past the marker at warp speed will lure them out.

The offshore waters have plenty of keeper-sized gag grouper, particularly in fall and spring when the fish move into 20- to 35-foot depths as the baitfish migrate.

HUDSON

The urban crunch spreading like cancer from Clearwater to the north hasn't quite invaded Hudson yet, and the fishery shows it. There are boats and boatmen, but nothing like the pressure that's common farther south.

The dozens of canals dredged to create waterfront homes here are all likely areas for winter snook, reds and trout, with the push inland usually coming in November. The fish stay until March, or until they're caught out, whichever comes first. Easy way to find the trout is to slow-troll a small jig or a shallow running plug such as the Rapala or Bangolure. Snook will usually take topwaters, but when they're moody, live shrimp or pinfish will do the job.

There's a public park and boat ramp just west of U.S. 19 which opens into Hudson Creek, and this is a good spot for a big snook after dark or early in the day on a large floater

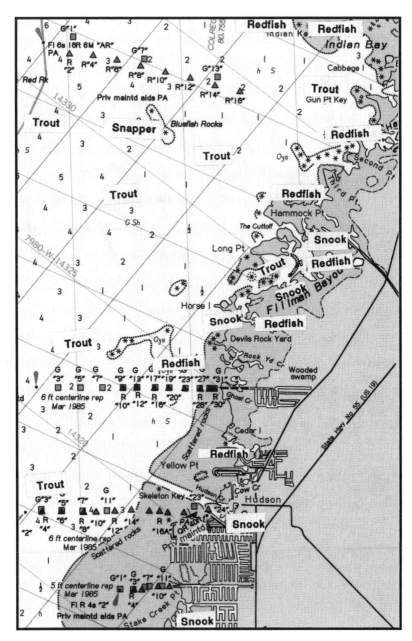

HUDSON TO ARIPEKA

the north side away from the boat ramp, as well as the swimming beach itself.

Fillman Bayou, Captain Dennis Royston's domain, is about two miles north of the Hudson Channel. It's long been a good redfish spot and has had a great snook fishery the last couple of years. This is about the farthest north that there are dependable numbers of snook on the west coast.

There are numerous grassy points that hold both species on rising water, while on the fall the fish move to the deeper swash channels. The middle of the bayou is grassy, and holds school-sized trout and an occasional spring cobia. The approach to Fillman across the flats is very shallow and studded with unmarked rocks--caution is advised.

There's a marked, dredged channel just south of Fillman where trout and reds gather in November and December at times. Jigs and live shrimp catch most of them. The oyster bars north of this channel are a good area to check for cruising reds in spring and summer on rising water.

ARIPEKA

Indian Bay, just north of the village of Aripeka, has shallow water and plenty of oyster bars, and holds redfish spring through fall. The 3- to 4-foot depths in the center sometimes have spawning trout in April and May. Follow the Aripeka Channel out to about marker 12 and turn either due north or due south and you'll find numerous rockpiles in about 3 feet of water--often good places to net scaled sardines. On high tides in spring, these sometimes attract schools of traveling bluefish. The whole area from here to Bayport is a minefield of unpredictable rocks out to about 3 miles offshore, and the inside waters tend to be extremely shallow, as in ankle deep--flats fishing is great, but this is a little too flat both for fish and for fishermen.

However, there's a dredged, 4-foot deep channel into Hernando Beach, and in early winter plenty of trout follow this route into the residential canals. A public ramp just west of State Route 595 provides access.

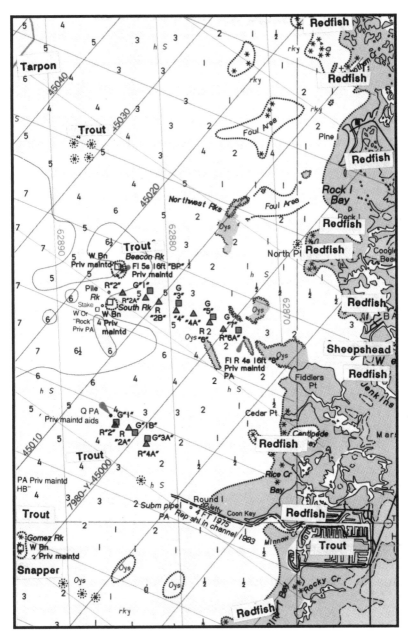

HERNANDO BEACH AND THE WEEKI WACHEE RIVER

WEEKI WACHEE

The structure changes a bit at the mouth of the Weeki Wachee River, due to the large volume of fresh water put out by this spring-fed river. There are more oyster bars, the first hint of the repetitive reef systems that are common from here northward.

There's a good ramp near the end of State Route 50 at Bayport, and this is the put-in point for many who visit the tarpon flats off Chassahowitzka since it lets into a deep, safe channel immediately. If you run out to the end of the markers, you'll find yourself in water about 5 to 7 feet deep with plenty of grass. Drift and cast, and you'll find trout, particularly in spring and fall. Nearer the shore around those abundant oyster bars is redfish country, particularly August through November. Pole and toss a gold spoon, soft jerkbait or topwater around North Point, Rock Island Bay, Higgenbothem Creek and Racoon Point.

West and northwest of the Weeki Wachee channel is an area of scattered rocks in 6 to 7 feet of water where you can often catch bait for offshore grouper forays, and sometimes in spring the grouper will come in to these areas to meet you. They also hold seabass, mangrove snapper and sometimes big trout or roving bluefish. Start with a noisy topwater tossed from long range, then work in closer with jigs or live bait.

In winter, lots of big sheepshead move well upriver in the warm waters of the river. Look for them in the rocky holes, and make long casts with sections of fresh shrimp or fiddler crabs.

CHAPTER 13

GULF GROUPER

Thanksgiving is the semi-official opening of inshore grouper action on the west coast, and anybody who loves bottom-bumping of the non-sexist kind will be out there sending pinfish on the journey of no return.

Grouper are caught in Florida waters year around, but in winter, the fish migrate inshore, often winding up on rockpiles where the water is only 20 to 40 feet deep. Along the central west coast, such rocks are found from 1 to 20 miles offshore, making them accessible to even the smaller saltwater boats on calm days.

One skipper who has mastered the art of trailing the grouper migrations is Captain Jim Bradley, formerly of Tampa, but now a riverside resident of Weeki Wachee.

FINDING THE HOTSPOTS

"The big secret," says Bradley, "is to work up your own set of numbers. Any numbers you find in a book or a magazine article are history, because it takes only a few boats to clean out a rock."

Captain Mel Berman of WFLA-970 Radio shows a healthy red grouper. Most are caught over "swiss cheese" bottom, areas with holes in flat, limerock strata.

How do you go about finding your own "numbers", or rockpiles identified by electronic loran coordinates?

The way Bradley did it was to spend a full year trolling the waters from Hudson to Homosassa. Pulling big diving plugs like the Magnum Rapala about 30 feet behind a planer, he patiently trolled map grids, working through a few miles a day, marking each spot where he caught fish on a chart, as well as recording the loran coordinates.

"At the end of that year, I not only had hundreds of good numbers, I had a chart that showed me entire areas where I knew the bottom was right, and where I knew the fish would be at a certain time of the year," Bradley recalls. "Fishing got easy after that."

BAIT AND TACKLE

The bait depends on the season according to Bradley. So long as the sardine migrations are still on, large or "horse" sardines are the preferred bait for most fishermen. But as the water cools, this bait disappears south, leaving only pinfish in local waters.

Fortunately, grouper like pins just as well as sardines-- and it appears that the larger gags prefer a big, darting pinfish year around.

Other effective baits include grunts and squirrelfish, and after the water cools, strips of bonito or other oily fish also seem to turn the fish on.

Dead bait including frozen sardines, cigar minnows and squid also catches some fish, but the frozen offerings don't stay on the hook as long and are not as appealing to the larger fish, says Bradley.

He likes stout tackle, essential to pull the bigger grouper away from their rock hideouts. Broomstick rods, revolving spool reels and 50 pound test line is favored. Hooks are 7/0, rigged with 4 to 8 ounces of lead, with the heavier weights used in deeper water when strong currents are running. The hook is attached to 3 feet of 100-pound-test mono, which provides a "handle" to boost fish aboard.

GROUPER GROPING

To work a spot, Bradley first marks it on his paper-graph depthfinder, tossing over a jug attached to a lead line when he sees a "spike" of fish rising up off a rock.

He then stops the boat and studies the wind and current, so that he can determine an "anchoring course" away from the buoy. The anchor must be set to put the stern of the boat over the fish. In 40 feet of water, he motors at least 200 feet upcurrent to drop the anchor, then backs down to the spot.

"Getting the anchor in the right spot is a big part of the game," says Bradley. "If you don't learn to do it just right, you'll never catch many fish--you can't be off by five feet and get them."

One trick that has made Captain Eric Coppin a top rod is casting the bait to explore adjacent pockets. It's no easy trick to sling a half-pound lead and a half-pound bait on a revolving spool reel, but Coppin says those who master it can usually catch the biggest fish of the day.

"You watch where the first fish you hook runs, and that's where the main rock is located," says Coppin. "Cast out that way and you'll usually hit the mother lode."

Bradley also notes that it takes patience to connect consistently.

"You might make 20 drops in a day, and maybe the fish are off at all of them except the last. Plan to spend the day out there and stay after it, and you'll bring home the limit almost every trip."

In fact, on our trip, the early drops produced only undersized grouper, those just short of the 20-inch minimum. There are now thousands of such fish in the Gulf, thanks to tight regulations put in place by the MFC. It's fun to catch them, but frustrating when you're looking for a platter of grouper fillets.

At about 3 p.m., as we were turning east for the ride back to Weeki Wachee, we tried a final rock, and that was the spot. The first drop produced a double, and by the time they had their 8-pound gags aboard I was wrestling a similar fish to the top. For the next 30 minutes, every pinfish that hit bottom was gulped by a grouper between 5 and 8 pounds.

LEAVE THEM BITING

We quit before the bite ended, at Bradley's suggestion.

"It's smart never to clean out a rock," he advised. "If you leave a few big fish on a spot, they attract more big fish. If you take all the big ones off, it's months before that spot produces big fish again."

Both reds and gags are far more abundant today than a few years back, thanks to the 20-inch size limit. The larger grouper are usually caught on live pinfish or grunts.

Though our fish were caught in somewhat deeper water, Bradley said that from Thanksgiving through winter, it's possible to catch jumbo grouper by free-lining baits over rocks so shallow that you can see their outline.

"They come up off the bottom in that situation, and you can catch them on light tackle. It's great sport," Bradley says.

WHERE TO FIND GROUPER

As Jim Bradley notes, consistently catching keepers is a matter of having a lot of secret spots that are found in YOUR little black book only. But, for those just getting started, the numerous artificial reefs placed by the Department of Natural Resources and others are a key to at least getting in the right neighborhood. The following list, provided by Florida Sea Grant, will provide you with plenty of action on mixed bottom fish and an occasional jumbo gag. Troll with wire line, downriggers or planers going to and from the reefs and you'll soon begin to develop your own list. Red grouper tend to be found in holes in the bottom, often between obvious rockpiles.

The listing is by county, with indications of the Loran C readings, the depth, the relief or height of the reef off bottom when available, and the distance from shore.

Name	Loran	Depth	Relief	Distance
HILLSBOROUGH COUNTY				
1. Port Manatee	14225.0/44557.4	21	13	.70
2. Bahia Beach	14245.4/44560.2	24	14	1.80
3. Picnic Island	14254.0/44619.4	26	?	1.00
4 Picnic Island Pier	14257.9/44648.5	18	8	0.09
5. Port of Tampa	14257.5/44632.3	24	12	0.60
6. Ballast Point	Adj. Pier	8	8	0.01
PINELLAS COUNTY				
1. St. Pete Beach	14192.9/44694.1	36	?	6.30
2. Treasure Island	14200.8/44738.7	33	?	5.80
3. Madeira Beach	14201.0/44768.0	33	?	5.70
4. St. Petersburg	14242,6/44615.6	36	?	1.00
5. Indian Shores	14200.1/44859.6	46	?	9.30
6. Blackthorn	14181.7/44942.7	80	?	12.80
7. D. T. Sheridan	14181.6/44943.3	80	?	12.80
8. Rube Allyn	14212.3/44886.4	50	?	9.20
9. Pier 60	14245.0/44916.0	12	?	0.01
10. Clearwater	14243.0/44861.5	29	?	3.30
11. Dunedin	14247.9/44887.3	30	?	4.40
12. Tarpon Springs	14259.3/44935.3	28	?	7.20
PASCO COUNTY				
1. Pasco No. 1	14275.8/45000.0	25	?	11.00
2. Pasco No. 2	14276.6/45050.8	40	20	13.20
3. Pasco No. 3	14274.8/45048.2	40	?	13.20
HERNANDO COUNTY				
1. A.H. Richardson	14325.3/45111.1	22	?	18.00
2. Jim Champion	14337.0/45160.0		?	17.00
CITRUS COUNTY				
1. Citrus County	14325.3/45305.5	30	10	19.20
LEVY COUNTY				
1. Cedar Key No. 2	14375.4/45466.4	26	?	11.00
2. Suwannee No. 1	14363.9/45540.0	39	?	16.80
3. Suwannee No. 3	14367.4/45566.4	35	?	17.50
4. Suwannee No. 5	14368.0/45595.0	38	?	18.40
5. Suwannee No. 7	14372.0/45614.4	34	?	18.00
6. Cedar Key No. 3	14375.0/45640.0	36	?	13.00
7. Cedar Key No. 1	14398.5/45549.3	23	?	9.00
8. Cedar Key No. 4	14388.0/45630.0	26	?	6.00
9. Coal Ash/Fla Pwr	14401.0/45535.0	25	?	9.30
10. Betty Castor	14410.4/45699.9	22	4	3.00

(Florida Sea Grant produces the "Atlas of Artificial Reefs", by Donald Pybas, annually. The book includes maps showing location of the various reefs and descriptions of their makeup. Copies are $6.36, to Florida Sea Grant College Program, Building 803, University of Florida, Gainesville, FL 32611.)

CHAPTER 14

CHASSAHOWITZKA TO HOMOSASSA

This area of the west coast is a unique estuary fed by gin-clear spring-rivers, all of them maintaining 72 degree temperature in their headwaters year around. We'll look at each river and its adjoining estuary separately.

THE CHASSAHOWITZKA FLATS

This is one of the smaller spring rivers, but the mangrove islands, creeks and flats at its mouth have some of the richest grass and most abundant fish.

The waters around Bird Island, aptly named for the huge number of frigate birds that nest there, frequently hold redfish in temperate weather. Black Rock Hole, about a mile west-northwest of Bird, is a 13-foot deep depression that often collects seatrout in fall. In summer, it's a noted spot for big tarpon, which lie under the floating grass and pick off floating crabs.

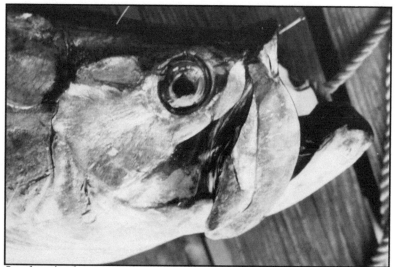

Jumbo-sized tarpon draw anglers from around the world to the flats off Chassahowitzka May through June each year. The giant fish are hard-pressed and difficult to hook, but many in excess of 150 pounds are jumped each spring.

Move out to 6-8 feet of water and you'll find scattered rockpiles that are good for some pan-sized mangrove snapper and sea bass. And, in spring, they sometimes hold a few keeper-size gag grouper, which will obligingly rise up to belt topwater plugs. Some of the rocks are indicated by asterisks on the chart, but many are not--and on low tide, some of them are just a foot under water so navigate with care.

The deep grass off Chassahowitzka tripod marker is also the center of much of the world-class fishing for giant tarpon that draws anglers from all across the nation beginning in late April and continuing through June. The fish are found from 3 to 8 miles out in water 5 to 12 feet deep. The fishing area extends roughly from Pine Island on the south to Chassahowitzka Point on the north. This is primarily fly-rod action, and it's essential to pole rather than try to motor up on the hard-fished silver kings. The fish are hard to see, harder still to fool. Definitely not a sport for beginners, but the experts regularly land fish here in excess of 150 pounds.

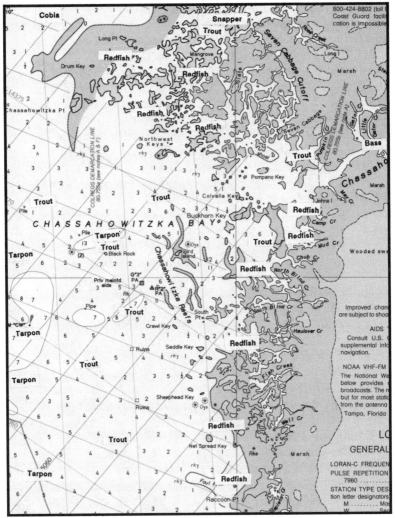

CHASSAHOWITZKA BAY

INSIDE CHASSAHOWITZKA POINT

Chassahowitzka Point is a good place to pole and sight-fish reds August through October--work in behind the islands on rising water, as well as out along the point, and check out the grass flats to the north of the point, as well. (This same area often holds cruising cobia in March and April--best lure is an 8-inch black plastic worm, the same thing freshwater bass anglers throw.)

There's a little more water as you move into the back country east of the point, and potholes in the region often hold some big trout on the first cool days of November.

For something a little different, run southwest from the point for about five to seven miles until you come into an area known as the "bird racks". There are old submerged poles here that once supported guano racks, where a cock-eyed plan to collect bird droppings as fertilizer went awry. These posts always hold snapper, and within a few hundred yards on either side there are usually hanging schools of yard-long houndfish that will readily belt a fast-moving jig. These guys have green flesh--they taste good, if you've got the nerve to eat something that looks so much like a snake.

If you have a shallow-draft boat and the ability to read the water, you might poke back into Blue Bay and Porpoise Bay, both hidden in the oyster bars and limerock islands northeast of Chassahowitzka Point. In March and April, a run of whopper black seabass sometimes settles into the deepest area of Blue Bay, where they'll readily take shrimp or jigs on bottom. All the waters in this area hold reds throughout the warmer months, and the deeper runs also hold some nice trout. It's finesse fishing, requiring silence and long casts, but you'll usually have the area all to yourself because most boatmen are scared off by the dangerous bottom.

While you're back in this country, you might run Seven Cabbage Cutoff, a narrow slough that runs from the Mason Creek basin to the Chassahowitzka basin, about three miles. It's not a particularly fishy flow because of the minimal depth, but it's an interesting ride where only the commercial well boats normally run. (Don't try this run if you draw more than 12 inches, and don't try it on low tide. Go on high water, with a high sun to allow you to see the numerous rocks.)

MASON'S CREEK

Mason's Creek, which runs out of the swamp south of Homosassa, is a blackwater creek, but its lower reaches are

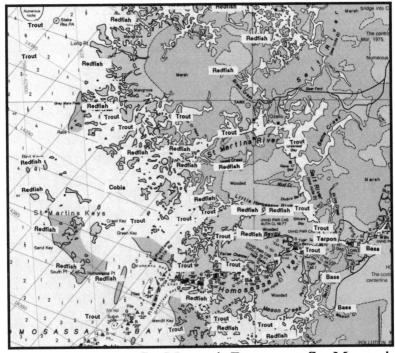

HOMOSASSA RIVER, ST. MARTIN'S RIVER AND ST. MARTIN'S KEYS

clear and hold large trout in April and again in October-- good spot to float a topwater with the tide. Fall redfishing is usually good, as well. Pay special attention to North Channel, which is deeper than the marked channel, and usually holds more fish. Throughout the area, extreme caution is necessary in running your boat, because there are hundreds of unmarked rocks and the bottom itself is limerock.

If you run upstream on Mason's Creek, you come to largemouth bass water. Fish the canals and creekmouths above Petty Creek on falling water with a Rapala and you'll catch plenty in the 1 to 2 pound class. There are also some 8-foot holes in the residential canals, and when the first frosts of winter come, these holes often fill up with big trout and reds.

In the bays on both sides of Chassahowitzka Point, cobia show up in March, often entering water only 3 feet deep. They frequently follow rays, and can be caught on large plastic worms or jigs.

The only two ramps in the Chassahowitzka area are within a couple hundred yards of where State Route 480 deadends. The spring boil where you launch is deep, but the river is too shallow for large boats on a low tide. Be cautious, particularly in winter when tides run lower than normal.

HOMOSASSA BAY

Homosassa Bay is grassy over much of its width, but the inside edges are rimmed with limerock ledges and unmarked rocks that require careful navigation.

The grass, in water from two to five feet deep, is a good place to drift in April and May and cast topwaters for seatrout. Pay particular attention to bars and channel edges--you might catch a cobia or a redfish on these spots, as well as trout.

There are finger channels both north and south of the main entry channel around markers 20 to 22 that usually hold trout in spring and fall.

THE HOMOSASSA RIVER

The Homosassa River gets a good run of tarpon from August through October, with the fish going all the way up to the entrance of Hall's River at times. In winter, the deeper holes around places like Hell's Gate and Tiger Tail Bay hold trout, reds, sheepshead and snapper, all best caught on live shrimp.

There's a little-known population of snook here, mostly caught on summer nights by fishing topwaters on falling tides around creek mouths in the upper Homosassa. You won't catch many, but the survivors here tend to be size XL.

The upper river, from Tiger Tail Bay landward, has pretty good largemouth bass fishing year around. Hall's River is a spring-fed tributary, also with good numbers of bass, though the clear water makes them difficult. Best lure is a small silver/black Rapala for school-sized fish, while a wild shiner about 6 inches long is best for the occasional big fish. It's not on a par with the bass fishing in most inland lakes, but it's a nice change from the saltwater diet.

OFFSHORE OF HOMOSASSA

There's excellent grouper fishing offshore of Homosassa in depths from about 28 feet out to 42 feet. Most anglers connect by trolling diving plugs on wire lines or planers.

There's also frequently "mud fishing" available in mid- to late November. This occurs when thousands of fish corner migrating shrimp and literally turn the water muddy as they root them out of the bottom. The mud may stretch for a mile or more, and it's usually fairly obvious due to birds whirling overhead. The muds are usually found on the outer edge of the grass flats, in 10 to 14 feet of water.

Drop a jig anywhere in a mud and it's instant fish, with anything from trout to silvers to grunts to sea bass and gag grouper likely to take hold. There are also usually big Spanish prowling the edges where the clear water meets the mud, and occasionally in these areas you may also have a big kingfish swallow a trout you're reeling in. It's a circus if you're lucky enough to find the action.

CHAPTER 15

HOMOSASSA TO CRYSTAL RIVER

This area is a clear water wonderland for flats anglers, though it can be a nightmare for deep-draft boaters who leave the marked channels. The fish get plenty of pressure, but thanks to the rich habitat, angling action holds on strong season after season.

THE LITTLE HOMOSASSA

The Little Homosassa and Sam's Bayou, both north of the main river, have numerous deep holes and bends, as does the Salt River, and many of them are good areas to probe for winter redfish, trout and mangrove snapper. Live shrimp is hard to beat, but 1/4 ounce bucktail jigs also work very well. There are oyster bars and holes at the mouth of the Little Homosassa, and if you approach these holes very quietly on low water, you can usually pick off some nice trout or reds on topwaters.

Best place to launch is at the public ramp in Old Homosassa, at the end of State Route 490. MacRae's Bait House is a Florida classic, where you can get all the necessary bait and tackle plus advice from folks who have spent their lives on the river. They also have pleasant accommodations. Riverside Villas, right next door, is a resort-style motel, and it also has a bait shop and boat ramp.

ST. MARTIN'S KEYS

The St. Martin's Keys, north of the Homosassa Channel, provide exceptionally clear, shallow water around their rocky shores, and there are nearly always redfish here. Unfortunately, there are also plenty of anglers, especially on weekends, so the fish are smart and spooky. Wading is the best way to get at them, and even then it usually takes long casts for good action.

St. Martin's River, which comes out of Ozello, is good along its edges for reds, good down the middle for trout, especially in fall and winter when the fish come inside. There's a public ramp in Ozello, and a couple of good little seafood restaurants.

The Salt River also runs past Ozello. It's an inside route from Homosassa to Crystal River, reasonably well-marked and with a minimum depth of 2 feet. There are holes down to 12 feet, and these holes can be great winter spots for trout and snapper.

There are a few deep holes in the bay between the mainland and St. Martin's Keys where you can catch an occasional cobia in spring and snappers in winter. Green Key Swash, a deeper, grassy area on the east side of St. Martins, is good for spring trout. So is Deep Creek, a little flowage just north of the mouth of the Homosassa. The Crows Nest Restaurant, right at the mouth of the river, is a good place for lunch within sight of some prime fishing waters.

CRYSTAL RIVER

This is the widest and deepest of the spring rivers along this portion of the coast, and it gets a strong run of trout and reds most years when waters cool in November.

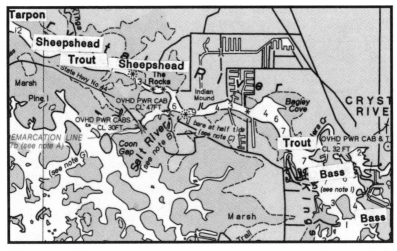

CRYSTAL RIVER

It's also a good spot for late summer tarpon, which are caught by trolling big spoons in the lower reaches, or by fishing cut mullet on bottom.

The upper mile of the river offers good and sometimes great largemouth bass fishing, but the water is jammed with weeds and only a few lures, including Limberneck type spinnerbaits, will get through the vegetation to get them. Rapalas also work well on high tides.

CRYSTAL BAY

Crystal Bay is dotted with oyster bars, and the ends of these bars have small passes with deeper basins on either side. Fish usually lie in the downtide basin--drift a topwater or an unweighted shrimp to them. There's also grass between the bars and more of it to the north, approaching the power plant spoil bars--all good topwater trout fishing from spring through late fall.

In spring and fall, pay close attention to the islands that stretch east from Mangrove Point, the archipelago south of the river mouth. This is a maze of winding creeks and hidden bays, and all of it is likely redfish water, with trout in the

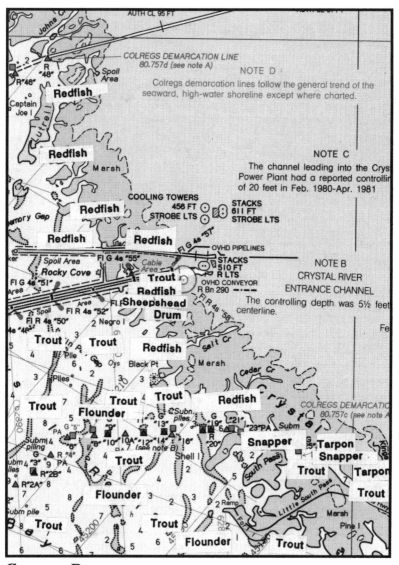

CRYSTAL BAY

150

deeper pockets. The stained water makes the gold spoon a good lure choice. On the outside, the grass around Gomez Rocks, with depths of 3 to 6 feet, always holds some trout in moderate weather--though it usually holds lots of anglers, as well. Work westward to deeper grass, keeping an eye out for muddy water or diving birds that might indicate a school. Quarter-ounce bucktails or plastic tailed jigs are the coin of the realm--make sure they're dredging bottom or you won't get many trout.

The spoil islands that extend from the powerplant, and those further north at the mouth of the Cross Florida Barge Canal, have deep cuts between them where you can connect with reds, trout, and jumbo jack crevalle on tide flows. Troll the edges of the deep channels with big diving plugs like the Bomber Long A or Magnum Rapala for whopper reds in fall. The outer end of the powerplant islands have a deep hole where jumbo reds nearly always school up in late August and on through September--live pinfish are the best offering there says local top gun Frank Schiraldi.

The powerplant itself is famed for holding some really large trout--in excess of 5 pounds--in winter, along with a lot of spinner sharks, sheepshead up to 8 pounds, jacks, etc., etc. Live shrimp, cut mullet, sinking plugs and jigs are all effective, best action usually from Thanksgiving to New Years. Note the outlet side is on the south--that's where the warm water exits. The pros at this location say the biggest trout are caught after dark on the first couple of freezing nights of the year.

Knox Bait House is the place to launch at the head of the river. Or, to avoid the low speed manatee zone, you can trailer west on State Route 44 and put in just beyond the swimming beach at the end of the road. It takes a careful eye to navigate away from this ramp because there are numerous unmarked shell bars, but you're in redfish country the minute you leave the ramp.

CHAPTER 16

WITHLACOOCHEE BAY TO WACCASASSA BAY

Now we're talking really secret spots, far from Florida's population boom. The area doesn't get a tenth the pressure of waters further south, and the fishing often shows it.

THE CROSS FLORIDA BARGE CANAL

The Cross Florida Barge Canal, just south of the Withlacoochee River, was a terrible boondoggle for tax payers, but for fishermen, not quite such a tragedy. The deepwater cut leading into the flats created a fishy highway that draws fish shoreward, particularly when the temperatures drop rapidly and the fish seek depth for warmth.

From October through January, trolling the canal with plastic tailed jigs or small diving plugs is a good way to locate the schools of trout. The fish sometimes move well inland, beyond the U.S. 19 bridge--and the rocky edges often hold schools of sheepshead and mangrove snapper in this period, too--live shrimp is the ticket.

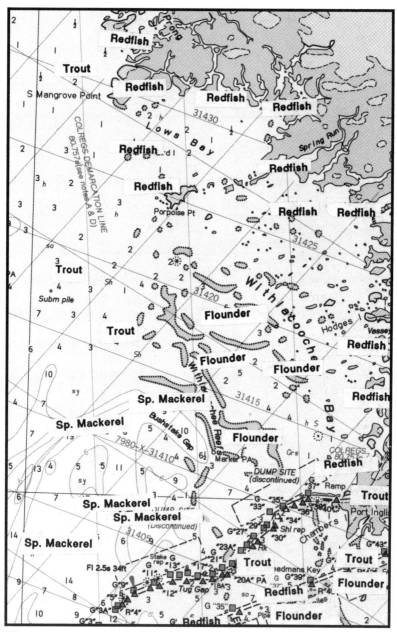

WITHLACOOCHEE RIVER AND WITHLACOOCHEE BAY

Topwaters around the oyster bars in this area produce some big trout in spring. The waters are shallow, rocky and risky, but for those with flat-bottomed boats and a willingness to explore, the bay offers excellent fishing and little competition.

Pulling bigger plugs like the Magnum Rapala will connect you with some whopper redfish, particularly in August, September and October. Those same months, and also in spring in April and May, are good times to toss noisy topwaters around the spoil bars on the south side of the channel. Don't crowd the bars too much, however--the fish are usually not right against the shore, but more often in the three to six foot depths on the edges.

THE WITHLACOOCHEE RIVER

The Withlacoochee River itself is a great winter fishery for reds, trout, snapper and sheepshead, with lots of fish in most of the deep, rocky holes. There are launching areas at the U.S. 19 Bridge, in the village of Yankeetown on the north shore, and at the river mouth, at the end of State Route 40.

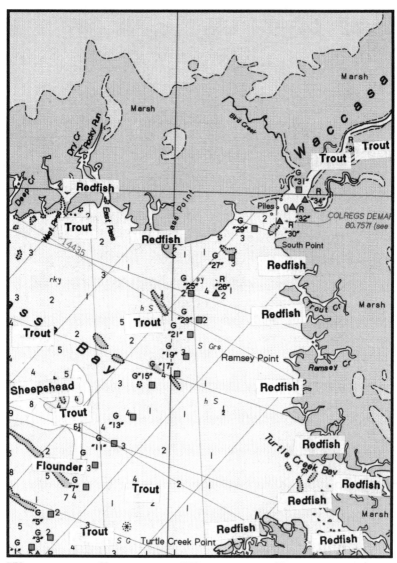

WACCASASSA RIVER AND WACCASASSA BAY

You don't even need a boat at the latter spot--in October, a run of reds often settles right into the basin in front of the ramp, where they can be caught on jigs or live shrimp.

The lower river also offers pretty good fishing for school-sized largemouth bass. Fish the creek mouths on falling tides with green Sluggos or Jerkworms or small Rapalas, all of which look a lot like needlefish, one of the primary foods in this brackish area.

WITHLACOOCHEE BAY

Withlacoochee Bay is notable for the Withlacoochee Reefs, a set of awesome oyster and limerock bars that run more or less north and south across the flow of the tides. There are holes 5 to 6 feet deep between them, and these often hold reds and trout in spring and fall.

Bushstake Gap, the first substantial water outside the reefs, has depths of up to 10 feet, and sometimes holds Spanish mackerel in April and again in October on the drops to the deeper water. This is also true for the tongue of deeper water leading into the gap--depths to 15 feet, small shoals to 4 feet make a good feeding area for the macks.

Turtle Creek Bay, south of the river mouth, is a good area to pole on rising water for redfish, as is Turtle Creek Point and Mangrove Point, working further south.

The islands and bars in Lows Bay are also likely for redfish, with the deeper water (about 3 to 4 feet on high water) likely to hold trout spring through fall.

Many of the narrow creeks inshore of this area have holes that hold reds and trout in winter, but the water is so shallow, particularly during coldfronts with northeast winds, that an airboat is the only safe way to get at them.

THE WACCASASSA

The Waccasassa is one of the few remaining rivers of any size in the state of Florida that has almost no human development. There's a boat ramp in the headwaters off State Route 326 south of Gulf Hammock--which is itself nothing but a crossroads. This is truly God's country, a wild, remote land where it's just you and the fish.

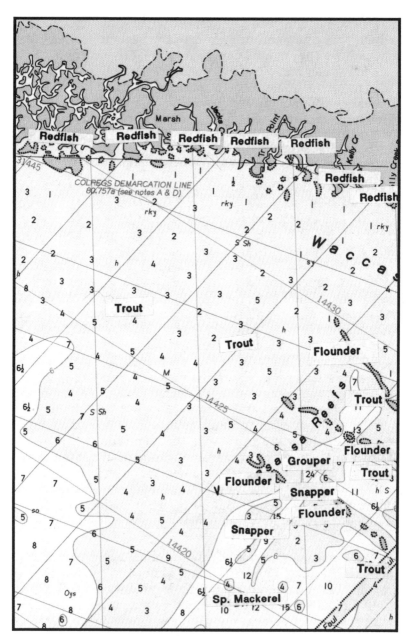

WACCASASSA BAY

158

Fortunately, there is a marked channel out of the river, or it's likely no one at all would ever fish Waccasassa Bay. It's guarded by the characteristic shell reefs of this area, row after row of them set across the main flowage, with holes as deep as 24 feet between the rows. Not surprisingly, these areas, just north of the marked channel, frequently produce good fishing for a bit of everything from cobia to grouper, snapper and seatrout.   Holes in the river and in Cow Creek, which makes off to the southeast near the mouth, often hold winter trout, reds, sheepshead, drum and snapper, all of which will eat a live shrimp on bottom.

With a flat-bottomed john boat, you can probe the north shore of Waccassasa Bay, which is riddled with small creeks where redfish prowl. The average depth along this entire shore is about 12 inches at mean low water, and there are lots of rocks, so go with caution if you go.

CHAPTER 17

CEDAR KEY TO SUWANNEE

Cedar Key is not quite so quiet as it was when I first discovered it 25 years ago. Back then, it was home only to commercial fishermen, and to hook-and-line anglers and duck hunters willing to travel for outstanding sport. These days, there are more artists and writers in town than fishermen, and some fear it may go the way of Key West, victim of its own picturesque aura as it becomes a playground for the wealthy tourist rather than an economy getaway for the angler.

But that hasn't happened yet, and except for the weekends, it's still pretty quiet ashore, without too much change in things except for a few more curio shops along the waterfront. Run your boat a half-mile in any direction and you step into Florida's past. There's zero development, and the waters are just as fishy as they used to be; probably better for some species thanks to better management.

THE CEDAR KEYS

Prime fishing gets rolling in April and May, with schools of big yellow-mouthed seatrout gathering to spawn over the

Redfish teem along the rocky shorelines and in the oyster-lined creeks of the Cedar Key area. Fishing is good year around, with a major surge in August and September.

sea grass and around the oyster bars. There's plenty of grass out in front of town, starting just beyond the main shipping channel and stretching around the islands off to the west. (Follow the markers very carefully--there's a 180-degree dogleg to the west and back, so don't try to cut the corner unless you can jump a foot-deep bar.

The public fishing pier downtown spans some of the deepest water in the area (14 feet) as it stretches out into the dredged ship channel, and there are always trout, drum, sheepshead and other finny critters around the pilings.

The city boat basin and excellent boat ramps are found downtown. You can tie up in the basin no matter what the weather and be protected from waves, because it's almost completely landlocked except for the shallow entry channel under a bridge. (That bridge keeps out boats with much superstructure, however.) Bigger boats can be launched directly into the Gulf on the southwest side of the street, just across from the basin.

CEDAR KEYS OVERVIEW

There are deep channels between all the main islands, with flats backing up each of the cuts. The area makes a wonderful highway for the fish, and loads of them use it. The flats south of Snake Key are often good for trout, as are those adjacent the channel on the south west side of Seahorse Key. The edges of all the channels are good on the rise for redfish, and you might find a cobia cruising in the same area from March through October.

From Northwest Channel, which cuts off the Main Ship Channel just west of town, you can take a deep-draft boat around South Bank and drift the 3- to 5-foot depths on the west side, where there are frequently trout on the grass patches. The edges of Deadman's Channel, between North Key and Sea Horse Key, is a redfish route in late fall, and also holds trout on the first chill of the year.

The grass runs for miles off to the north, all the way to Steinhatchee. There's so much water and so few anglers here, compared to the massive pressure exerted in areas like Tampa Bay, that the trout fishing remains super, maybe Florida's best.

THE INSHORE REEFS

However, navigation is definitely demanding. The Suwannee Reefs extend northwest about two miles from the marshy shoreline, and if you don't know where to cut across them you can lose a lower unit--they go dry on low water. Easy way to cross is via Derrick Key Gap, which is well-marked and has 3-foot depths--it begins about a mile due north of the number 3 marker on Northwest Channel. Once you're through the gap, ease in on push pole or trolling motor to fish the back of the Suwannee Reefs for reds and big trout, or drift the 6-foot-deep basin of Suwannee Sound for school trout.

The gaps in Lone Cabbage Reef, about a mile from the shoreline here, are also likely spots for reds and jumbo jack crevalle.

A jig, slow-sinking plug or a topwater dropped anywhere over the grass is likely to draw fish during this period, including a few big ones to 4 pounds, though the average spring trout here runs about two pounds.

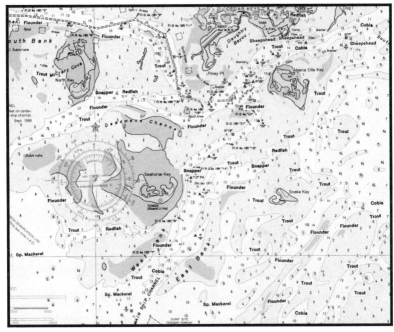

The Cedar Keys

Shell bars like sprawling Corrigan's Reef, northeast of Cedar Key and Lone Cabbage, Half Moon and Suwanee Reefs to the northwest, are good for some larger trout in spring also. All of these areas are surrounded by water that's 3 to 5 feet deep, but the shell reefs themselves go dry halfway to low tide. The remaining water pours through the gaps, and so do the baitfish, so the gamefish wait there for them.

Since redfish became gamefish several years ago, there has been excellent redfishing inshore around the holes, mangroves and oyster bars throughout the spring for anglers tossing jigs and gold spoons. Redfishing has always been spectacular here. Before they became gamefish, one net fisherman caught over 5,000 pounds in a single set on one hole. The nets kept them pretty well trimmed off until the closure, but these days it's common to nail a trout on one toss, a red on the next, and if you get back into the oyster-

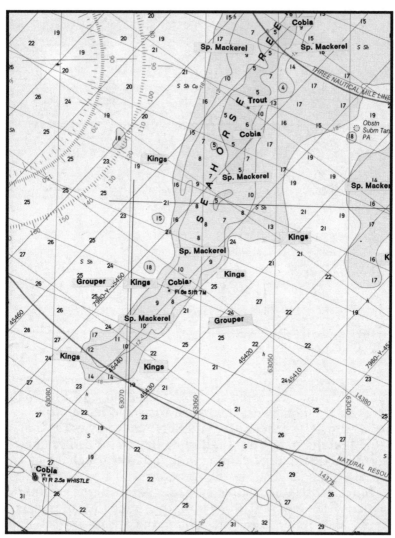

SEAHORSE REEF

166

The inshore reefs composed of rock and shell hold lots of crabs and baitfish, and are natural magnets for redfish. Try cuts through the bars on tide changes.

lined creeks and holes, the reds usually beat the trout to the lures--50-fish days are not uncommon.

SEAHORSE REEF

If you fish the deeper grass in spring, you'll also connect with Spanish mackerel regularly. They're part of a massive run that gathers at Seahorse Reef, a spit of sand and grass jutting 10 miles into the deeper water, beginning in April. The fish are around the bar all summer and into October.

Seahorse is also a great place to troll for king mackerel, with the big guys usually off the bar a bit in water 18 to 20 feet deep. The jumbos run to 30 pounds, and these are best taken by slow-trolling a threadfin or mullet. School kings to 12 pounds or so hit spoons and jigs towed rapidly, sometimes on downriggers or planers, sometimes near the surface.

You'll occasionally see bluefish chopping up bait on top off the tip of the bar here, and maybe bonito a bit further out as well. It's a great place to fish, unique in all the Florida gulf.

A nice thing about Seahorse, for first-time visitors, is that you can't miss it. It lies right beside the marked ship channel, so you simply follow the markers to the action.

SUWANNEE SOUND

Fall is good for everything, with trout and redfish moving into the dozens of creeks north of Cedar Key on the back side of Suwannee Sound. The entire shoreline in this area is lowland marsh, and there's a creek every quarter-mile or so. Places like Shired Creek, Bumblebee Creek, Johnson Creek, Clark Creek and many unnamed flowages all have redfish holes in them. It's shallow, dangerous water, but with patience and a push pole, you can reach into some true wilderness and enjoy great fishing.

Just don't get over-confident once you leave the creeks and break back out on the sound. In some areas, the shell bars poke through the surface as much as two miles from the nearest shoreline.

THE SUWANNEE

Winter trout fishing can be phenomenal in the lower Suwannee. Trout, redfish, sheepshead and a bit of everything else stack up in the lower reaches after the first freeze.

West Pass and East Pass, the two largest branches of the flow with holes down to 20 feet, usually hold the fish.

Anglers work their lures downstream or across the current. There are lots of snags on the bottom so you need heavy line to avoid losing lots of lures. Most work plastic-tailed jigs or bucktails in the 3/8 to 1/2 ounce range right on bottom, or ease sinking lures like the 52M MirrOlure along just off bottom. Live shrimp or small baitfish weighted adequately to reach bottom are also effective.

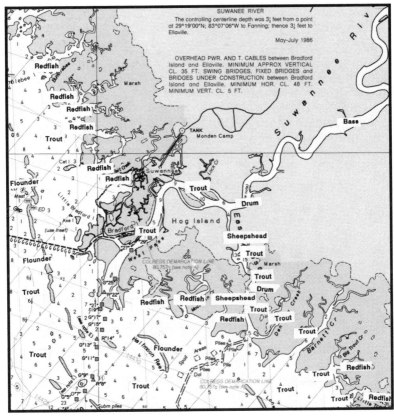

THE SUWANEE RIVER

Barnett Creek and Dan May Creek, both south of East Pass, have depths of 9 feet or more, and often hold winter fish as well. Moccasin Creek, running into Hog Island between East Pass and West Pass, also produces.

The action remains good until it gets really cold in January. State Route 349 runs to the village of Suwannee off U.S. 19, where there are boat ramps, marinas, restaurants and hotels that cater to anglers.

There's outstanding grouper fishing off Suwanee, anywhere from 20 feet on out. If you don't have local numbers, pull a planer and a diving plug until you connect, then mark the spot and return to fish it with live pinfish.

CHAPTER 18

WEST COAST GUIDES

While chartering a boat or hiring a guide looks like a considerable investment to those of us who must work hard for our discretionary dollars, it can often be money well spent. A professional angler is on the water every day, knows where the fish are in each season of the year and what foods they're eating, and can teach you more in one trip than you're likely to learn in weeks on your own.

Most guides specialize both by area and by species. Those listed here as "inshore" specialize in fishing the estuaries for trout, reds, snook and tarpon, at rates from $250 to $400 per day. Those listed as "offshore" for the most part specialize in offshore fishing for grouper and king mackerel, at rates around $500 per day. A few specialists also offer trips to the edge of the continental shelf, usually over several days, to troll for marlin, wahoo, tuna and other pelagics. The rates run $600 and up for up to six anglers.

There are also numerous "party boats" in the St. Petersburg-Clearwater area, which specialize in 4- to 8-hour trips carrying 30 or more anglers for bottom fishing at prices beginning as low as $35. These trips usually produce grunts,

Guides like Capt. Earl Waters spend countless hours on the water and can take you to the fish on any given day. The fee paid for their expertise is money well invested.

seabass and mangrove snapper, but occasionally turn up some large grouper and king mackerel as well.

Everett Antrim, Port Richey, inshore (813) 868-5747
Larry Blue, St. Petersburg, inshore/offshore (813) 595-4798
Jim Bradley, Weeki Wachee, inshore/offshore (904) 596-5639
Herb Brown, Tarpon Springs, inshore (813) 797-2731
Charlie Cleveland, Tampa, inshore (813) 935-0241
Ray DeMarco, Anna Maria, inshore (813) 778-9215
Al Dopirak, Crystal Beach, inshore (813) 785-7774
Mike DuClon, Tarpon Springs, inshore (813) 937-9737
Double Eagle Party Boat, Clearwater, offshore (813) 446-1653
Henry Edwards, Tampa Bay, inshore (813) 831-4207
Paul Hawkins, St. Petersburg, inshore (813) 894-7345
Richard Howard, Clearwater, inshore/offshore (813) 446-8962
Hubbard's Party Boats, Madeira Beach, offshore (813) 393-1947
Van Hubbard, St. Petersburg, inshore (813) 697-6944
Ky Lewis, Clearwater, offshore, (813) 442-1502
Mike Locklear, Homosassa, inshore (904) 628-2602
Dave Markett, Tampa Bay inshore (813) 962-1435
Tim McOsker, St. Petersburg, inshore (813) 797-7715
Larry Mendez, Tampa, inshore (813) 874-3474
Bill Miller, Homosassa, inshore (813) 935-3141
Dave Mistretta, St. Petersburg, offshore (813) 595-3276
Scott Moore, Cortez, inshore (813) 778-3005
Abbie Napier, Cedar Key, inshore (904) 543-5511
Jack Powell, St. Petersburg, inshore/offshore (813) 345-1606.
Bill and Anna Rae Roberts, Cedar Key, inshore (904) 543-5690
Dennis Royston, Hudson, inshore (813) 863-3204
Frank Schiraldi, Crystal River, inshore (813) 795-5229
Russ Sirmons, St. Petersburg, inshore (813) 526-2092
Tim Slaught, Homosassa, inshore (904) 628-5222
Tom Tamanini, Tampa Bay, inshore (813) 581-4942
Chris Turner, St. Petersburg, offshore, (813) 367-1268
Earl Waters, Homosassa inshore, (904) 628-0333
Shorty Welch, St. Petersburg, offshore (813) 392-3554
Bruce Williams, Crystal River, inshore (904) 795-7302
James Wisner, Tampa Bay, inshore (813) 831-5659
James Wood, Terra Ceia, inshore (813) 722-8746
Dave Zalewski, Largo, offshore, (813) 393-5475

Larsen's Outdoor Publishing
FISHING & HUNTING RESOURCE DIRECTORY

If you are interested in more productive fishing, hunting and diving trips, this information is for you!

Learn how to be more successful on your next outdoor venture from these secrets, tips and tactics. Larsen's Outdoor Publishing offers informational-type books that focus on how and where to catch the most popular sport fish, hunt the most popular game or travel to productive or exciting destinations.

The perfect-bound, soft-cover books include numerous illustrative graphics, line drawings, maps and photographs. Many of our LIBRARIES are nationwide in scope. Others cover the Gulf and Atlantic coasts from Florida to Texas to Maryland and some foreign waters. One SERIES focuses on the top lakes, rivers and creeks in the nation's most visited largemouth bass fishing state.

All series appeal to outdoors readers of all skill levels. Their unique four-color cover design, interior layout, quality, information content and economical price makes these books your best source of knowledge. **Best of all, you will know how to be more successful in your outdoor endeavors!!**

Great Tips and Tactics For The Outdoorsmen of the Nineties!

BASS SERIES LIBRARY
by Larry Larsen

(BSL1) FOLLOW THE FORAGE VOL. 1 - BASS/PREY RELATIONSHIP - Learn how to determine dominant forage in a body of water and you will consistently catch more and larger bass.

(BSL2) VOL. 2 BETTER BASS ANGLING TECHNIQUES - Learn why one lure or bait is more successful than others and how to use each lure under varying conditions.

(BSL3) BASS PRO STRATEGIES - Professional fishermen know how changes in pH, water level, temperature and color affect bass fishing, and they know how to adapt to weather and topographical variations. Learn from their experience. Your productivity will improve after spending a few hours with this compilation of techniques!

(BSL4) BASS LURES - TRICKS & TECHNIQUES - When bass become accustomed to the same artificials and presentations seen over and over again, they become harder to catch. You will learn how to modify your lures and rigs and how to develop new presentation and retrieve methods to spark the interest of largemouth!

(BSL5) SHALLOW WATER BASS - Bass spend 90% of their time in the shallows, and you spend the majority of the time fishing for them in waters less than 15 feet deep. Learn productive new tactics that you can apply in marshes, estuaries, reservoirs, lakes, creeks and small ponds, and you'll likely triple your results!

(BSL6) BASS FISHING FACTS - Learn why and how bass behave during pre- and post-spawn, how they utilize their senses when active and how they respond to their environment, and you'll increase your bass angling success! By applying this knowledge, your productivity will increase for largemouth as well as redeye, Suwannee, spotted and other bass species!

(BSL7) TROPHY BASS - If you're more interested in wrestling with one or two monster largemouth than with a "panful" of yearlings, then learn what techniques and locations will improve your chances. This book takes a look at geographical areas and waters that offer better opportunities to catch giant bass. You'll also learn proven lunker-bass-catching techniques for both man-made and natural bodies of water!

(BSL8) ANGLER'S GUIDE TO BASS PATTERNS - Catch bass every time out by learning how to develop a productive pattern quickly and effectively. "Bass Patterns" is a reference source for all anglers, regardless of where they live or their skill level. Learn how to choose the right lure, presentation and habitat under various weather and environmental conditions!

(BSL9) BASS GUIDE TIPS - Learn secret techniques known only in a certain region or state that often work in waters all around the country. It's this new approach that usually results in excellent bass angling success. Learn how to apply what the country's top guides know!

Nine Great Volumes To Help You Catch More and Larger Bass!

LARSEN ON BASS SERIES

(LB1) LARRY LARSEN ON BASS TACTICS is the ultimate "how-to" book that focuses on proven productive methods. It is dedicated to serious bass anglers - those who are truly interested in learning more about the sport and in catching more and larger bass each trip. Hundreds of highlighted tips and drawings explain how you can catch more and larger bass in waters all around the country. This reference source by America's best known bass fishing writer will be invaluable to both the avid novice and expert angler!

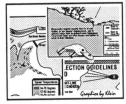

BASS WATERS SERIES
by Larry Larsen

Take the guessing game out of your next bass fishing trip. The most productive bass waters in each Florida region are described in this multi-volume series, including boat ramps, seasonal tactics, water characteristics and much more. Both popular and overlooked locations are detailed with numerous maps and photos. The author has lived and fished extensively in each region of the state over the past 25 years.

(BW1) GUIDE TO NORTH FLORIDA BASS WATERS - Covers from Orange Lake north and west. Includes Lakes Orange, Lochloosa, Talquin and Seminole, the St. Johns, Nassau, Suwannee and Apalachicola Rivers and many more of the region's best! You'll learn where bass bite in Keystone Lakes, Newnans Lake, St. Mary's River, Doctors Lake, Black Creek, Juniper Lake, Ortega River, Lake Jackson, Lake Miccosukee, Chipola River, Deer Point Lake, Blackwater River, Panhandle Mill Ponds and many more!

(BW2) GUIDE TO CENTRAL FLORIDA BASS WATERS - Covers from Tampa/Orlando to Palatka. Includes Lakes George, Rodman, Monroe, Tarpon and the Harris Chain, the St. Johns, Oklawaha and Withlacoochee Rivers and many others! You'll find the best spots to fish in the Ocala Forest, Crystal River, Hillsborough River, Conway Chain, Homosassa River, Lake Minneola, Lake Weir, Lake Hart, Spring Runs and many more!

(BW3) GUIDE TO SOUTH FLORIDA BASS WATERS - Covers from I-4 to the Everglades. Includes Lakes Tohopekaliga, Kissimmee, Okeechobee, Poinsett, Tenoroc and Blue Cypress, the Winter Haven Chain and many more! You'll learn where bass can be caught in Fellsmere Farm 13. Caloosahatchee River, Lake June-in-Winter, Lake Hatchineha, the Everglades, Lake Istokpoga, Peace River, Crooked Lake, Lake Osborne, St. Lucie Canal, lake Trafford, Shell Creek, Lake Marian, Myakka River, Lake Pierce, Webb Lake and many more!

> For more than 20 years, award-winning author Larry Larsen has studied and written about bass fishing. His angling adventures are extensive, from Canada to Honduras and from Cuba to Hawaii. He is Florida Editor for *Outdoor Life* and contributor to all major outdoor magazines.

OUTDOOR TRAVEL SERIES
by Larry Larsen and M. Timothy O'Keefe

Candid guides with inside information on the best charters, time of the year, and other important recommendations that can make your next fishing and/or diving trip much more enjoyable.

(OT1) FISH & DIVE THE CARIBBEAN - Vol. 1 Northern Caribbean, including Cozumel, Cayman Islands, The Bahamas, Jamaica, Virgin Islands and other popular destinations. Required reading for fishing and diving enthusiasts who want to know the most cost-effective means to enjoy these Caribbean islands. You'll learn how to select the best destination and plan appropriately for your specific interests.

(OT3) FISH & DIVE FLORIDA & The Keys - Includes in-depth information on where and how to plan a vacation to America's most popular fishing and diving destination. Special features include artificial reef loran numbers; freshwater springs/caves; coral reefs/barrier islands; gulf stream/passes; inshore flats/channels; and back country estuaries.

(OT2) FISH & DIVE THE CARIBBEAN - Vol. 2 - *COMING SOON!* Southern Caribbean, including Guadeloupe, Costa Rica, Venezuela, other destinations.

> "Fish & Dive the Caribbean, Vol. 1" was one of four finalists in the Best Book Content Category of the National Association of Independent Publishers 1991 competition. Over 500 books were submitted by various U.S. publishers, including Simon & Schuster and Turner Publishing, Inc. Said the NAIP judges "An excellent source book with invaluable instructions for fishing or diving. Written by two nationally-known experts who, indeed, know what vacationing can be!"

DIVING SERIES
by M. Timothy O'Keefe

(DL1) DIVING TO ADVENTURE will inform and entertain novice and experienced divers alike with its in-depth discussion of how to get the most enjoyment from diving and snorkeling. Aimed at divers around the country, the book shows how to get started in underwater photography, how to use current to your advantage, how to avoid seasickness, how to dive safely after dark, and more. Special sections detail how to plan a dive vacation, including live-aboard diving.

> M. Timothy O'Keefe was editor of the first major dive travel guidebook published in the U.S. The award-winning author writes for numerous diving, travel and sportfishing publications.

COASTAL FISHING GUIDES

(FG1) FRANK SARGEANT'S SECRET SPOTS - Tampa Bay to Cedar Key - A unique "where-to" book of detailed secret spots for Florida's finest saltwater fishing. This guide book describes little-known honeyholes and tells exactly how to fish them. Prime seasons, baits and lures, marinas and dozens of detailed maps of the prime spots are included. A comprehensive index helps the reader to further pinpoint productive areas and tactics.

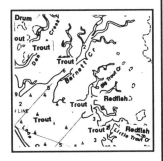

(FG2) FRANK SARGEANT'S SECRET SPOTS -Southwest Florida
COMING SOON!!

INSHORE SERIES

by Frank Sargeant

(IL1) THE SNOOK BOOK-"Must" reading for anyone who loves the pursuit of this unique sub-tropic species. Every aspect of how you can find and catch big snook is covered, in all seasons and all waters where snook are found.

(IL2) THE REDFISH BOOK-Packed with expertise from the nation's leading redfish anglers and guides, this book covers every aspect of finding and fooling giant reds. You'll learn secret techniques revealed for the first time. After reading this informative book, you'll catch more redfish on your next trip!

(IL3) THE TARPON BOOK-Find and catch the wily "silver king" along the Gulf Coast, north through the mid-Atlantic, and south along Central and South American coastlines. Numerous experts share their most productive techniques.

(IL4) THE TROUT BOOK -Jammed with tips from the nation's leading trout guides and light tackle anglers. For both the old salt and the rank amateur who pursue the spotted weakfish, or seatrout, throughout the coastal waters of the Gulf and Atlantic.

Frank Sargeant is a renown outdoor writer and expert on saltwater angler. He has traveled throughout the state and Central America in pursuit of all major inshore species. Sargeant is Outdoor Editor of the Tampa Tribune and a Senior Writer for *Southern Saltwater* and *Southern Outdoors* magazines.

HUNTING LIBRARY

by John E. Phillips

(DH1) MASTERS' SECRETS OF DEER HUNTING - Increase your deer hunting success significantly by learning from the masters of the sport. New information on tactics and strategies for bagging deer is included in this book, the most comprehensive of its kind.

(DH2) THE SCIENCE OF DEER HUNTING - Covers why, where and when a deer moves and deer behavior. Find the answers to many of the toughest deer hunting problems a sportsman ever encounters!

(TH1) MASTERS' SECRETS OF TURKEY HUNTING - Masters of the sport have solved some of the most difficult problems you will encounter while hunting wily longbeards with bows, blackpowder guns and shotguns. Learn the 10 deadly sins of turkey hunting and what to do if you commit them.

FISHING LIBRARY

(CF1) MASTERS' SECRETS OF CRAPPIE FISHING by John E. Phillips - Learn how to make crappie start biting again once they have stopped, how to select the color of jig to catch the most and biggest crappie, how to find crappie when a cold front hits and how to catch them in 100-degree heat as well as through the ice. Unusual but productive crappie fishing techniques are included. Whether you are a beginner or a seasoned crappie fisherman, this book will improve your catch!

OUTDOOR ADVENTURE LIBRARY

by Vin T. Sparano, Editor-in-Chief, <u>Outdoor Life</u>

(OA1) HUNTING DANGEROUS GAME -It's a special challenge to hunt dangerous game - those dangerous animals that hunt back! Live the adventure of tracking a rogue elephant, surviving a grizzly attack, facing a charging Cape buffalo and driving an arrow into a giant brown bear at 20 feet. These classic tales will make you very nervous next time you're in the woods!

(OA2) GAME BIRDS & GUN DOGS - A unique collection of stories about hunters, their dogs and the upland game and waterfowl they hunt. These tales are about those remarkable shots and unexplainable misses. You will read about good gun dogs and heart-breaking dogs, but never about bad dogs, because there's no such animal.

LARSEN'S OUTDOOR PUBLISHING
CONVENIENT ORDER FORM
ALL PRICES INCLUDE POSTAGE/HANDLING

FRESH WATER
___ BSL3. Bass Pro Strategies ($14.95)
___ BSL4. Bass Lures/Tech. ($14.95)
___ BSL5. Shallow Water Bass ($14.95)
___ BSL6. Bass Fishing Facts ($13.95)
___ BSL8. Bass Patterns ($14.95)
___ BSL9. Bass Guide Tips ($14.95)
___ CF1. Mstrs' Scrts/Crappie Fshg ($12.95)
___ CF2. Crappie Tactics ($12.95)
___ CF3. Mstr's Secrets of Catfishing ($12.95)
___ LB1. Larsen on Bass Tactics ($15.95)
___ PF1. Peacock Bass Explosions! ($16.95)
___ PF2. Peacock Bass & Other Fierce
         Exotics ($17.95)
___ PF3. Peacock Bass Addiction ($18.95)

SALT WATER
___ IL1. The Snook Book   ($14.95)
___ IL2. The Redfish Book ($14.95)
___ IL3. The Tarpon Book ($14.95)
___ IL4. The Trout Book ($14.95)
___ SW1. The Reef Fishing Book ($16.45)
___ SW2. Masters Bk/Snook ($16.45)

REGIONAL
___ FG1. Secret Spots-Tampa Bay/
         Cedar Key   ($15.95)
___ FG2. Secret Spots - SW Florida ($15.95)
___ BW1. Guide/North Fl. Waters ($16.95)
___ BW2. Guide/Cntral Fl.Waters ($15.95)
___ BW3. Guide/South Fl.Waters ($15.95)
___ OT3. Fish/Dive Florida/ Keys ($13.95)

HUNTING
___ DH1. Mstrs' Secrets/ Deer Hunting ($14.95)
___ DH2. Science of Deer Hunting ($14.95)
___ DH3. Mstrs' Secrets/Bowhunting ($12.45)
___ DH4. How to Take Monster Bucks ($13.95)
___ TH1. Mstrs' Secrets/ Turkey Hunting ($14.95)

OTHER OUTDOORS BOOKS
___ DL2. Manatees/Vanishing ($11.45)
___ DL3. Sea Turtles/Watchers' ($11.45)

FREE BROCHURES
___ Peacock Bass Brochure
___ LOP Book Catalog

BIG MULTI-BOOK DISCOUNT!
2-3 books, SAVE 10%
4 or more books, SAVE 20%

INTERNATIONAL AIRMAIL ORDERS
Send check in U.S. funds; add $6 more for 1 book, $4 for each additional book

ALL PRICES INCLUDE U.S. POSTAGE/HANDLING

No. of books _____ *x $*_____*ea*   =   *$*_____
No. of books _____ *x $*_____*ea*   =   *$*_____
    Multi-book Discount   (%)   *$*_____
SUBTOTAL   *$*_____

☐ **Priority Mail (add $2.50 more for every 2 books)** $_____
   TOTAL ENCLOSED (check or money order) $_____

*NAME*_____ *ADDRESS*_____

*CITY*_____ *STATE*_____ *ZIP*_____

Send check/Money Order to: Larsen's Outdoor Publishing,
Dept. BR99, 2640 Elizabeth Place, Lakeland, FL 33813
(Sorry, no credit card orders)

WRITE US!

If our books have helped you be more productive in your outdoor endeavors, we'd like to hear from you! Let us know which book or series has strongly benefited you and how it has aided your success or enjoyment. We'll listen.

We also might be able to use the information in a future book. Such information is also valuable to our planning future titles and expanding on those already available.

Simply write to Larry Larsen, Publisher, Larsen's Outdoor Publishing, 2640 Elizabeth Place, Lakeland, FL 33813.

We appreciate your comments!

Larry Larsen

OUTDOOR SPORTS SHOWS, CLUB SEMINARS and IN-STORE PROMOTIONS

Over the course of a year, most of our authors give talks, seminars and workshops at trade and consumer shows, expos, book stores, fishing clubs, department stores and other places. Please try to stop by and say hi to them. Bring your book by for an autograph and some information on secret new hot spots and methods to try. At these events, we always have our newest books, so come and check out the latest information. If you know of an organization that needs a speaker, contact us for information about fees. We can be reached at 813-644-3381. At our autograph parties, we talk "outdoors" and how to enjoy it to the fullest!

Save Money On Your Next Outdoor Book!

Because you've purchased a Larsen's Outdoor Publishing
Book, you can be placed on our growing list of
preferred customers.

You can receive special discounts on our wide selection of
Outdoor Libraries and Series, written by our
expert authors.

PLUS...

Receive Substantial Discounts for Multiple Book Purchases

AND...

Advance notices on upcoming books!

Yes, put my name on your mailing list to receive

1. Advance notice on upcoming outdoor books
2. Special discount offers

Name_____

Address_____

City, State, Zip_____

Index